FLEET WALKER'S DIVIDED HEART

Biography
lends to death
a new terror.

Oscar Wilde

FLEET WALKER'S DIVIDED HEART

The
Life of
Baseball's
First Black
Major
Leaguer

DAVID W. ZANG

University of

Nebraska Press

Lincoln & London

Library of Congress Cataloging-in-
Publication Data
Zang, David.
   Fleet Walker's divided heart : the
life of baseball's first Black major
leaguer / David W. Zang.
      p.   cm.
   Includes bibliographical references
(p.   ) and index.
   ISBN 0-8032-4913-6 (alk. paper)
   1. Walker, Moses Fleetwood,
b. 1857.   2. Afro-American baseball
players—United States—Biography.
3. International League of Baseball
Clubs.   4. Baseball—United States—
History—19th century.   I. Title.
GV865.W34Z35   1995
796.357′092—dc20   94-33517
[B]   CIP

TO JOANIE

CONTENTS

. . . .

ILLUSTRATIONS

Map, Northeastern United States, xviii

Following page 70

Oberlin College's first varsity team, 1881

Scoresheet from 1881 season

Tappan Square, Oberlin College, c. 1875

Weldy Walker, 1883

Moses Fleetwood Walker, 1883

Toledo Blue Stockings, 1883

Major league Toledo squad, 1884

J. D. Shibe Company advertisement, 1884

The White Stockings, 1888

The Syracuse Stars, 1888

Walker's exploding artillery shell

Fleet and Ednah Walker's Opera House, c. 1910

The Cadiz Opera House, c. 1949

. . . .

ACKNOWLEDGMENTS

I confess to having had the biographer's fantasy of discovering the secret diary of my subject. Moses Fleetwood Walker was a good candidate to have kept one, but if he did so, it is still at large. Thankfully, in its absence, many people helped my efforts to uncover the details of his story and keep its interpretation on course. If I veered at times, the mistakes are mine. With gratitude, I would like to acknowledge the people who assisted this work.

The largest debt I owe is to Jerry Malloy, a baseball researcher who has done extensive and fine work on Walker. In an unprecedented act of generosity, Jerry shared not only his thoughts on Walker, but his entire file of documents. They arrived at a point long after I thought this manuscript was complete. Their availability added detail and insight that would have been otherwisc lacking. I am grateful beyond words to Jerry and the researchers who sent him material over the years. I hope the book does justice to his contribution.

Similarly, University of Arkansas professor Willard B. Gatewood Jr., author of the fine *Aristocrats of Color,* exceeded all the bounds of mere courtesy. In response to my queries about an important issue, Professor Gatewood sent me all of his original notes on the subject. I thank him for his trust and generosity.

I extend my sincere gratitude to these interviewees for sharing their candid remembrances with me: Marcella Ballard, Esther Clark, James Johnson, Ruth Minteer, and Dennis Palmer Jr., Fleet Walker's grandnephew.

My friends Elliott Gorn, Miami University of Ohio, and Randy Roberts, Purdue University, read drafts of the manuscript and made suggestions that improved it; Dave Wiggins, George Mason University, over the years encouraged the project, passed along thoughts and material, and accompanied me on trips to the National Archives.

My research was made considerably easier by the cooperation and involvement of a number of repositories and their staffs: the Oberlin College Archives, especially Roland Baumann, Tammy Martin, and Brian Williams; the Harrison County (Ohio) Historical Society, especially Charles Wallace; the Bentley Historical Library, at the University of Michigan, especially Nancy Bartlett and Greg Kinney; the National Archives in Washington DC, especially Wayne Cook, Bill Creech, Walter Hill, John Vernon, and Reginald Washington; the National Baseball Hall of Fame and Museum; the Jefferson County Historical Society and the Schiappa Library, both in Steubenville, Ohio; and the Case Western University law library. Thanks also to Grace Abernethy, of Steubenville's Union Cemetery; Gary J. Arnold, Ohio State Historical Society; Richard J. Behles, Health Sciences Library, University of Maryland at Baltimore; Beverly Braskett, Supreme Court of Ohio; Mickey Cochrane, of Oberlin College's John Heisman Club; Jim Danky, Wisconsin State Historical Society; Steve Gietschier, archivist for *The Sporting News;* Sharon Mollock, of Towson State University's Cook Library; Don Ritchie, U.S. Senate Historical Office; John Robert, historian for the Federal Bureau of Prisons; Rev. Lloyd Smith, Historical Society of Mount Pleasant, Ohio; Beverly Watkins, Great Lakes regional branch of the National Archives; Jack Webster, historian for the Toronto Police Department; and Beverly Zona, Lawrence County (Pennsylvania) Historical Society.

Special thanks to Robert W. Peterson, whose excellent book, *Only the Ball Was White,* first alerted me to the intrigue of Fleet Walker; to David Paccone, who ran down much crucial material in Syracuse; and to John McLucas, Towson State University, who translated Latin for me. Thanks also to Mark Hirsch, Tony Kraus, Robert Osterhoudt, and Edward Schnoor for efforts that in one important way or another helped me to conceptualize and reshape this manuscript. To interested and supportive friends and family, thank you.

. . . .

INTRODUCTION

... there can be given no sound reason against race separation. All experience and every deduction from the known laws and principles of human nature and human conduct are against the attempt to harmonize two alien races under the same government.

Who would have imagined that the first black major league baseball player harbored such views on American race relations? Bitterness may have leaked from some of the reflections Jackie Robinson offered in retirement, but his life was public testament to hope and progress – integration, not segregation. Of course, Jackie Robinson knew that he was not the first black big leaguer, just the first of the modern era. He knew that nearly seventy years earlier there had been another, a man who had been the first to play in the majors and then the last to play in either the major leagues or the International League until Robinson himself. That man was Moses Fleetwood Walker. A mulatto born before the Civil War, Walker lived through the late nineteenth and early twentieth centuries in defiance of social convention. When he authored his separatist lines in 1908, he had been out of baseball for nearly twenty years. That year he proposed that all American blacks return to Africa – be returned by force if necessary. In historical terms, Walker's call for exodus was scarcely a murmur, but in emotional terms it was the sound of a tormented heart finally splitting in two.

Walker was an intellectual man, and the imagery of a divided heart may seem incongruous at first consideration. Ever since Sigmund Freud dared to build a hangman's scaffolding out of the inner fears and secrets of the human mind, biographers have been quick to spring the trapdoor on their subjects, and it would seem an easy matter in Walker's case. Not only did he present a classic case of masked anger, he did so at a time when public confidence in the assertions of science was fueling interest in and acceptance of research like Freud's. The antiseptic language of psychiatry could never, however, have captured the source or essence of

Walker's emotions. For while his rage may have peaked in Freud's heyday, it took root before the Civil War and matured amid the emotional sensibilities of the Victorian era. Walker's own book on the history of the Negro race, written to accompany his African emigration plans, attempted to explain his frustrations through an appeal to the canons of scientific thought and educated conjecture. But it ultimately revealed a man unable to escape a complex reality: that individuals react to an emotional context deeper than the reach of science and to a cultural context greater than the sum of personal neuroses — to things, that is, that can only be described as matters of the heart.

Being alert to contradictions is a requirement for understanding "Fleet" Walker. Paradox is central to his story. His life was full of difficult choices, each one seeming to add to the cumulative gulf between who he was and who it seemed he ought to have been. Perhaps this owes to the underlying fact that Walker was unable to recognize some of the demons that chased him toward despair, and simply unable to defeat many of those he did recognize. Whatever the reasons, Walker seldom failed to confound. Though his vivid life was entwined with and aware of the historical record, it seemed to run always a step ahead of the collective consciousness that became the core of that record.

The trail leading to Walker lacks the voluminous documentation and the cultural signposts that mark Jackie Robinson's saga and might have been lost long ago but for the horde of baseball lovers that has trampled it in Robinson's wake. While Walker's status as the first black major leaguer — a title that bears an indictment of American society at large and dubious honors for the black population — has invited nearly universal mention of and comparison to Robinson, it has at least kept Walker from slipping through the cracks of time. Both stories are important ones. Walker and Robinson had some common experiences, but while Robinson played at a time when the historical tide was carrying society toward integration, Walker stood as a nearly solitary figure attempting to play ball as an ebb tide swept away popular support for racial equality.

Still, it is fitting that race and baseball would figure in bringing his story to light. The baseball establishment was, even in the late nineteenth-century, consciously defining the game as a quintessential American institution, one that would later be instrumental in forcing social integration. Indeed, many baseball lovers have come to regard the game's initial hostility toward Robinson as merely the natural reluctance of an early courtship that blossomed inevitably into a courageous embrace. Of course, integration has done little to ease racial tensions. And if baseball merits credit as a powerful cultural force, then the game's mythologists should admit that making an icon of Robinson has been inadequate penance for baseball's more significant role in undercutting, in Fleet Walker's day, American notions of what constitutes a fair and civilized society. Mythmaking, of course, can afford little stock in reality.

There is this indisputable reality of American life: we always make too much of race, or too little, but never, it seems, just the right amount. Perhaps it can be no other way. If there is one thing more absurd than linking personal behavior to rational thought, it is trying to make sense of the centuries of emotional wreckage, intellectual anguish, economic drain, and misspent energy that the race issue has wrung from both whites and blacks. Walker's life amplified the absurdities. The complex of interrelated variables – class, education, family life, talent – that affected his life were all tied to the changing views of Americans on race – or more accurately, color. His light complexion slid him back and forth along the scale of social acceptability as American attitudes toward the mixing of white and black bloodlines shifted over time. Further, his uncertain place in the middle invited the scapegoating barbs of both whites and blacks who viewed the center from opposite ends. In an attempt to resolve his dilemma, Walker tried to present the intercontinental transplantation of millions of native citizens as a rational proposal, all the while knowing that, while it was not reasonable, it was at least as rationally defensible as the caste system that had supported slavery and then segregation. The realization must have been maddening. Even as he argued for race separation, he nonetheless continued the struggle to harmonize his Anglo and Negro aspects. He admired and hated white society; he quite possibly loathed his African heritage even more.

While racially inspired self-hatred is not a new theme in African-American or ethnic studies, it is always a sobering and fretful one, and its presence in Walker invites the discovery of some of the synapses that join collective emotion and individual behavior. The task has always been both the blessing and bane of biography. Two writers have offered observations that provide valuable insight on the fragile relationship between historical forces and personal choices. As he weighed the impact of Elvis Presley on American culture, Greil Marcus noted that "the question of history may have been settled on the side of process, not personality, but it is not a settlement I much appreciate. Historical forces might explain the Civil War, but they don't account for Lincoln; they might tell us why rock 'n' roll emerged when it did, but they don't explain Elvis any more than they explain Little Peggy March."[1] And in a recent essay on the meaning of Malcolm X, Gerald Early, in addressing the complex struggle blacks face in trying to reconcile their African and

American aspects, wrote that "we must accept who and what we are and the forces and conditions that have made us this, not as defeat or triumph, not in shame or with grandiose pride, but as the tangled, strange, yet poignant and immeasurable record of an imperishable human presence."[2]

The themes of division and paradox offer a framework, but they do not explain Moses Fleetwood Walker. In attempting to remove himself from the particular and harsh realities of his own existence, Walker sought to locate his rage in the broader stream of social movements and generalities. The ironic result was that though he tried to defy prejudice, Walker often ended up feeding many of the old fears and stereotypes that whites held for mulattos and blacks. He becomes understandable to us, then, only in the terms of Marcus and Early. For though he advocated radical disjuncture rather than reconciliation, and though his life illustrates certain historical trends and illuminates certain moments, and though he is to some both a heartbreaking and broken-hearted symbol of the most tragic and enduring battle in American history, Moses Fleetwood Walker was above all, like Elvis, Malcolm, Jackie, and each of us, an immeasurable and imperishable human presence.

FLEET WALKER'S DIVIDED HEART

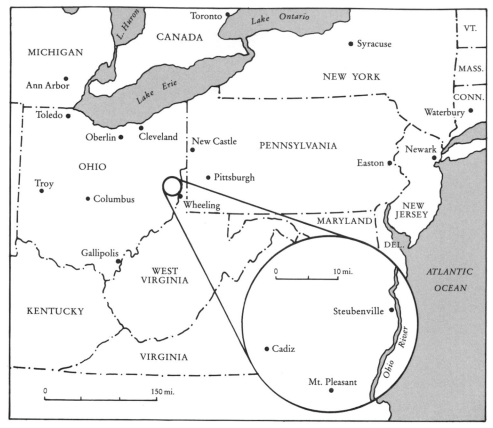

This map of the Eastern United States includes Fleet Walker's homes, the towns and cities he represented while a ballplayer, and other places of importance in the story of his life.

1

. . . .

EARLY MOSAIC

It is fall 1880, and at Oberlin College, in Ohio, a group of students is conspiring every afternoon to break the windows in Cabinet Hall. The students regard this classroom building, like other structures on the Oberlin campus, as part of the natural landscape that defines their baseball fields. The windows of Cabinet Hall beckon irresistibly to batters. But they beckon from a tantalizing distance, and the lack of a single shattered pane has stretched across too many sunlit afternoons and turned the quest into an obsession of heroic failure. On this particular October day the windows are mocking the best athletes the school has ever seen, taunting a group that includes at least four students who will eventually play the game professionally. One of this group, Fleet Walker, has been at Oberlin for nearly three years, his lean, muscled body refining the possibilities for hitting a baseball long distances, his flair for the dramatic fueling his determination to do the impossible. Though he was once a good student, Walker has begun skipping classes on a regular basis, forgoing the classroom for the baseball diamond. In a moment of perfect metaphor for his life, Fleet Walker becomes a first. He is the first to conquer Cabinet Hall – but not its windows. With one legendary swing, one still recalled fifty years later by an Oberlin alumnus, Walker hits a ball that sails clear over the building. Naturally, the bases are loaded.[1] It is a grand slam of epic proportions, but a drive that nonetheless avoids its target, a majestic near miss whose roots in futile grandeur run back to his birth – and beyond.

> Monday's child is fair of face,
> Tuesday's child is full of grace,
> Wednesday's child is full of woe,
> Thursday's child has far to go . . .

On 7 October 1857 – a Wednesday – Caroline Walker expelled the fifth of her six (or seven) children from the safety of the womb. Until later in his life, however, when the woe would reveal itself in the form of guns, knives, alcohol, and vitriol, it was not apparent that this child, Moses Fleetwood Walker, belonged to any one day. In fact, depending on one's willingness to sacrifice reality to superstition, it might have appeared that Caroline, a midwife, used the nativity as a practicum and elected to give birth across the first four days of the week. For as sure as he carried a full measure of woe, Fleet Walker was unquestionably fair of face, full of grace, and possessed of an ambition that would banish his dreams to distant places. By the end of his sixty-seven years, Walker had overwhelmed the simplistic prophecies of the nursery rhyme to such an extent that the possibility of a four-day birthing could not be dismissed out of hand. This Wednesday's child had become by turns a law student, a professional baseball player, an inventor, an activist, an author, an entrepreneur, a killer, and a felon. He had done so with a divided heart that tugged his extraordinary life back and forth between boundless promise and utter despair, between paragon and paradox.

His divided nature was insured, and the despair and paradox foreshadowed, the moment he was born as a light-skinned mulatto – the hybrid result of white and black relations. Of all the gaps that separated Americans in 1857 – between North and South, city and country, rich and poor – none was more conclusively divisive than that between black and white. Being a mulatto meant serving as chafing evidence that someone had breached that gap in the most intimate – or most violent – of ways. Befitting Walker's fractious and unpredictable life, the search for the transgressors in his past must wind through a complex mix of childhood influences. The place in which he was born, the area in which he was raised, his name, his father's works, and the specter of slave ancestry all lent their own shading to the inescapable and defining reality of his skin color.

One thing is certain. Fleet Walker was not the direct offspring of black and white. His parents were themselves mulattos. His father, Moses W. Walker, was born in 1820. When history first took note of him, recording his marriage to Caroline O'Harra on 11 June 1843,[2] he was residing in eastern Ohio's Jefferson County. In 1850 the couple was settled in Mount Pleasant, a small town tucked into the county's southwest corner. Moses was working as a cooper, or barrel maker, to support a family that had begun sprouting in 1844, the year after his marriage to Caroline. Cadwallader, the first son, had been followed by William (born 1845), Mary (1849), and Sarah (1851).[3] When Fleet came along in 1857, the Walkers were living at the foot of a hill in the shadow of a large Friends meeting house, and in the larger shadow cast by the town's outsized reputation for opposing slavery.

A strategic location and an extensive Quaker community made Mount Pleasant a vital place in eastern Ohio at the time of Fleet's birth. The town appears to visitors of the late twentieth century as an American Brigadoon, emerging suddenly and briefly from the rounded green hills and narrow valleys that shield it from modern intrusions. But in the midnineteenth century just the Ohio River and fifteen miles of hills and forests separated Mount Pleasant from the slave market of Wheeling (West) Virginia, from slave hunters and their hounds, and from American citizens who felt vastly different about human chattel.

Though its population was less than one thousand, Mount Pleasant hummed with the work of blacksmiths, cabinetmakers, printers, tanners, shoemakers, hatters, tailors, and even a few factories. The only commercial staple not to be found was liquor, an absence that owed to Quaker temperance. If the abstinence dampened social life, it did not kill it entirely. Twice a year, festive weeklong meetings of Ohio Quakers jammed the rutted roads leading into Mount Pleasant with carriages as far out as four miles.[4]

Beginning around 1815, the antislavery sympathies of the Quakers had also made the roads into Mount Pleasant essential to runaway slaves who traveled over them and stopped in the village during their journeys to freedom. Because many of Jefferson County's early settlers were antislavery New Englanders and Quakers from Pennsylvania and North Carolina, the number of slaves escaping through the region was larger than in most other areas of Ohio, itself the most popular state of destination for fugitive slaves.[5] The physical barrier that the Ohio River placed between freedom and the slave hunters also wooed runaways to eastern Ohio. Though nearly all of the state's towns would become stops on the Underground Railroad, those in the east formed an early and lively trail that ran from Pittsburgh to the northwest.[6] Some of Mount Pleasant's large, stately homes had concealed spaces and false floors for hiding runaways, and, according to area lore, the nearby Hanes Mill sat atop a tunnel through which many slaves passed to freedom.

The heavy traffic on Mount Pleasant's Underground Railroad was a contentious issue among the town's Quakers. Active participation was unsettling to some because it meant violation of fugitive slave laws and necessitated lying to authorities. Individual Friends who played important parts in the network freed their consciences by refusing to acknowledge that any person could be a slave and consequently a fugitive runaway. Despite differences concerning the Underground Railroad, however, Mount Pleasant's Quakers agreed in principle to opposition to slavery and found additional outlets for activism.

In 1817 a Mount Pleasant Quaker had begun publishing *The Philanthropist,* a newspaper that was the nation's first to advocate abolition. Another paper from Mount Pleasant, the *Genius of Universal Emancipation,* published in 1821, was the first devoted entirely to abolition. Both papers were conversant with the infant colonization schemes being proposed for America's free blacks. Ohio's first abolitionist meeting convened in 1837 in Mount Pleasant. In 1848 the Mount Pleasant Free Produce Company of Ohio opened a store that banned the sale of slave-made goods.[7] All were part of the area's active resistance to slavery, a conspiracy that had to become paradoxically bolder yet quieter in the case of former slaves who decided to settle in Jefferson County rather than continue northward.

The Ohio River, because it attracted runaway slaves, was also fertile and exciting territory for slave hunters and their dogs, and Black laws passed by the Ohio legislature in 1804 required proof of free title for blacks crossing the state line.[8] Until the outcome of the Civil War made one's origins moot, it was in the interest of all blacks to claim free states as their places of birth. Less than ten miles from Mount Pleasant there was a unique community of manumitted Virginia slaves, "industrious and strong at church-going."[9] Known to area residents as Hayti, this colony on the McIntyre Creek was begun in 1829 when a white man gave the land to his daughter and her husband, a former slave. Though the Moses Walker family lived among the ninety blacks who made up about one eighth of the population of Mount Pleasant proper,[10] not Hayti, they were part of a network of familiarity that existed among the county's blacks. While those in Hayti might flaunt their freedom, it was best for others in the area to live with unasked questions about questionable pasts and with a willingness to defend anyone's assertions as everybody's truths. This strategy of silence composes part of the historical veil that covers the roots of Fleet Walker's family tree. The documents that allow historians to lift the veil high enough for a peek underneath only add pieces to an unsolvable puzzle.

Moses Walker came to Ohio from Pennsylvania, likely a beneficiary of Quaker sympathies and patronage. Among the Quaker families of Washington County in western Pennsylvania who migrated due west into the Mount Pleasant area were Cadwalladers. Either a broom maker or cabinetmaker of that name could explain the name of the Walkers' firstborn.[11] Still, it is plausible that Moses began life in Virginia, if not as a slave then as a mulatto child in a state hostile to race mixing. In later years census takers recorded Pennsylvania as the state of his birth, with two important exceptions. In 1870 – after the war – his home state was listed as Virginia. More baffling was the claim by daughter Mary in the 1910 census that her father had been born in Canada.[12]

The census cannot place him in either Pennsylvania or Virginia prior to 1850, but if he was a namesake there were just two men who might have fathered him: a free black tradesman who resided alone in Virginia's Brunswick County at the time of the 1840 census or a white Presbyterian minister in Pennsylvania's Washington County. The prospect that the latter was Fleet Walker's grandfather, though improbable on the surface, is an intriguing possibility. The minister's household contained at least six children, and though all were listed as white, it seems unlikely that if he sired an illegitimate son by a black woman that he would reveal him to the census taker. Additionally, the 1880 census claimed that Moses Walker's mother came from Virginia and his father from Pennsylvania. Such a circumstance would strengthen contentions that his parents could have been the white minister and a black mistress with whom the son lived. Later in life, Moses expanded the puzzle once more when he himself turned to the ministry.[13]

As for Fleet's mother, Caroline, born in 1822, all editions of the census agree on Ohio as her birthplace. Nonetheless, her place in the family history is not without controversy. One document, the 1937 death certificate of the youngest Walker sibling, Weldy, lists his mother's maiden name as Maria Simpson. As Moses and Caroline raised all the Walker children under the same roof, the recording may have been a simple error, though one repeated in Weldy's newspaper obituary and by a number of people who later wrote about Fleet Walker. Still, given the trouble that would eventually split their marriage and the later relationships of its children, it is not unthinkable that the last of these children was born to a different mother. No Maria Simpson appears in the censuses of Jefferson County, but an intriguing entry in the 1920 census finds James Simpson, a thirty-year-old Virginia-born steel laborer, as one of just two boarders living with Weldy Walker at Steubenville's Union Hotel. The final oddity is that the hotel was run by Fleet Walker's son,

5
. . . .
Early Mosaic

Thomas, the informant who supplied the name of Maria Simpson to the coroner's office in 1937. When asked for the maiden name of Fleet's mother fifteen years earlier, Thomas had told the coroner he did not know it. Was he finally letting slip a family secret in 1937? And was the secret that Caroline O'Harra was not the mother of Weldy, or was it perhaps that Maria Simpson had been Caroline's slave name?[14]

While both of Caroline's parents were from Virginia,[15] and the O'Harra surname suggests either ties to slavery or a close connection to white kin, the record is mute on both counts. One person who drew on former acquaintances to tell Fleet Walker's story in the midtwentieth century claimed that both Moses and Caroline had been slaves, but the account was so grossly inaccurate in other details as to make the assertion suspect.[16] If Caroline or her husband were once slaves, it was a fact passed along within the family and one that was lost with the family's passing. If they were former slaves from Virginia, however, one more touch of irony would surround Fleet's birth. The folklore of the African Asante, a tribe represented among Virginia's slave population, held, like the English nursery rhyme, that one's day of birth foretold one's character. In the Asante scheme, Wednesday's children were "quick tempered, aggressive and troublemakers."[17] Whether the Walkers were vested in either Anglo or African folk belief, it is foreboding that the two cultures that would pull his heart in opposing directions agreed that the timing of his birth signaled a difficult future.

If the Walkers were not among the runaway slaves who surged into the area in the years between 1840 and the Civil War, the abolitionist sentiment of Mount Pleasant nonetheless impressed itself upon them with great weight. The dedication of Moses to Negro issues was, in fact, gathering steam at the time of Fleet's birth. The evidence lies not only in the activism that would later run through Fleet's adult life, but in the profound consciousness that suddenly marked the family's selection of names.

African tradition was to name children for all four grandparents. Many blacks, however, several generations removed from Africa, had begun to follow the eighteenth-century Virginia pattern of naming the first or second son for the father. Moses Walker had followed neither tradition in naming his first two sons Cadwallader and William. Moses Fleetwood was the third Walker son, yet the first to take the father's name. A century later, psychological literature would note the degree to which some parents bestow names in the hope that they will magically endow their children with special qualities. Some researchers even theorize that once an object acquires an assigned name, it must take on the properties that are viewed as functions of that name.[18] Moses did not know this literature, of course, but as a black man who had lived with the name for thirty-seven years in antebellum America, he must have known better than most what a huge weight he was strapping to his newborn's back when he named him.

Moses. The implications of the name are many and large. Certainly black Americans prior to the Civil War knew its significance. Slaves, whose heads held a patchwork quilt of biblical history, American history, and African remembrance, associated the name Moses with all great historical events. Their deliverance from the suffering of slavery loomed as the greatest of all. Indeed, their desire for freedom from bondage – either in heaven or on earth – drove them to assimilate the images of Jesus and Moses into one messianic figure.[19] It further caused them to regard an array of leaders as the flesh-and-blood incarnations of their anticipated liberator. Some of the chosen, as with Abraham Lincoln and Harriet Tubman, held obvious qualifications; some, like South Carolina's onetime Republican candidate for governor Franklin J. Moses, offered mostly the promise of a name. Through the time of the Emancipation, the idea of a Moses who would lead blacks to freedom remained a fervid, if mythic, hope. With the end of the Civil War, the need for a liberator waned, but the hardships of Reconstruction and Jim Crow segregation would trigger the search again. Additionally, the figure sought after at the turn of the century would become not merely a Moses *for* the black population, but a Moses *of* the black population – literally a Black Moses. Between 1880 and 1920 a number of men would bear the title. Among them were Henry M. Turner, Marcus Garvey, and Mifflin Wistar Gibbs, the "Black Moses of the West." Throughout his life, Moses Fleetwood Walker variously identified himself as Moses, Moses F., or Fleet. Ironically, in the document that would (in his sixth decade) publicly advocate a return to Africa for all American blacks, he chose M. F. as his pen name, a designation that seemed to beg for distance from his biblical namesake and the weight of becoming the real Black Moses.

Though the significance of his middle name, Fleetwood, is indeterminable, the younger Moses was commonly known by early adulthood by its shortened version, Fleet. There has been speculation that the family bestowed the nickname during his childhood to lessen the confusion of having a Moses as both father and son in the same house. Perhaps, but it may also have provided, at least during periods of his life, a respite from the demands of the name Moses and a more suitable self-image. The Bible often uses the idea of the transformation of one's identity through name alteration, and *Fleet* came to aptly characterize both the speed associated with Walker's later rise in professional baseball and the well-tailored style for which he became known throughout life. As ballplayer and dandy, his identity as Fleet reflected a transformation from the seriousness that the name Moses carried.

Whether Moses W. Walker had intended to offer blacks a child who would take literally the demands of his name, he and Caroline certainly considered the naming process a serious and deliberate undertaking. Just two years after Fleet's birth they named their fourth son Weldy Wilberforce, combining a biblical form of the word *wealthy* — and perhaps a deliberate derivation of abolitionist Theodore Weld's name, or possibly the family name of Jefferson County's pioneering Alexander Welday — with the surname of the famed English abolitionist, William Wilberforce.

Although Fleet Walker spent less than three years in Mount Pleasant, the significance of the town and the circumstances of his birth, his name, and his family background are undeniable. They all contributed to unsettled possibilities and future complications in forging an identity. They were forces that would sometimes not become apparent for years, and that sometimes would submerge and resurface across the decades ahead. But they all acted in concert to heighten the devastating impact of the larger reality that was with him always, that rubbed unceasingly against his many talents and desires, summoning instant challenges to his native intelligence, physical sturdiness, industry and thrift, sexual appetite, and ethical behavior. The reality that most confounded his sense of wholeness, cursed him more deeply with each passing year, and eventually wore through to his soul was that Fleet Walker was unavoidably and irrevocably the product of both Negro and Caucasian blood.

Later in the century the census would attempt to carefully define and sort mulattos (three-eighths to five-eighths Negro), quadroons (one-fourth Negro), and octoroons (one-eighth Negro). When the federal government decided to first use the mulatto category of identification in 1850, however, it instructed its census takers, in the interest of "important scientific results," to regard as mulatto "all persons having any perceptible trace of African blood."[20] In 1850, then, the designation *mulatto* marked Moses W. and Caroline Walker as simply people of African ancestry. Genealogical proofs aside, however, it seems likely that one — or both — of them were not far removed from the source of mixed blood. Photographs of Fleet and brother Weldy show them to be light-skinned with a measure of what have come to be defined as Caucasian features. Descriptions of Fleet early in his professional life labeled him a quadroon, and a later reference to the daughters of Fleet's sister, Mary, identified them as "voluptuous quadroons."[21]

The burden of being a mulatto reverberated in Fleet Walker's later words of self-negation. "It is impossible to make a hybrid race of men," he would write in 1908. At the time, he had been exposed for five decades to the misguided work of social theorists intent on separating white and dark-skinned Americans into races. That their erroneous findings could eventually convince a scholarly, critical thinker like Walker is testimony to how pervasive and persuasive their campaign had been. It was already in full swing during his childhood.

While some scientists of the midnineteenth century undertook the study of racial meaning with good intentions, many race theorists were busy turning those good intentions into elaborate rationalizations that connected so-called racial characteristics to the low social standing of American Negroes. Working like canal diggers, these theorists sought routes as direct as possible and dug the channels only as deep as necessary. Deriding the Enlightenment view that held human skin color to be a short term result of climatic and environmental conditions, these midcentury theorists believed either that the various races were created separately to inhabit the earth's varying geographical areas or — to accommodate Darwin's assertion of a single creation for all humankind — that the races had over the centuries developed distinct traits that constituted permanent and irreversible racial differences.

The idea of distinct racial heredity held sway during most of Fleet Walker's lifetime. While elsewhere in North America a person's social standing and racial identity depended on a number of factors, including skin color, anatomical features, and hair texture, in the United States blood was perceived as the vital source of racial distinction. The belief that blood contained the seeds of differing traits between the races was an attractive one for race theorists because it grounded race distinctions in an immutable biological fact.[22] When the blood was not mixed, the theorists had little trouble in attaching the labels *superior* and *inferior* to the races.

Separatist theorists seized upon available research findings to advance their faith in the superiority of whites to all other races. Several government agencies had become involved during the Civil War with the widescale measurement of Union soldiers. The U.S. Sanitary Commission had conducted a study that considered body dimensions, head size, vision, teeth, strength, respiration, and pulmonary capacity. The conclusion was that Negroes were distinctly inferior to whites, a finding that Edward D. Cope, a respected paleontologist at the University of Pennsylvania, would later elaborate on as evidence of the Negro's close structural resemblance to anthropoids.[23]

More influential was the wartime study of Sanford B. Hunt, a surgeon in the U.S. Volunteers. His autopsies of soldiers revealed the Negro brain to be five ounces lighter, on average, than the white brain. At nearly the same time, a German anatomist noted that shape and characteristics caused the adult Negro brain to approximate that of "the child, the female, and the senile white."[24] Brain measurement would grow increasingly sophisticated by century's end, but even in the 1860s it was enough to reinforce a primary contention of race theorists: that the blood carried not only physical traits, but also those of intelligence, culture, and character. The virtues and the vices of a race, once acquired, could be transferred biologically and then "become thoroughly inbred in the stock."[25]

Though their ruminations selectively and intentionally pinched reality into a shape that fit their own desires, these theorists and their popularizers were successful in implanting the idea of race hierarchy in the public mind. While Confederate President Jefferson Davis's belief in a version of separate race creation was predictable, Abraham Lincoln's views were not. In an 1858 debate the future emancipator contended that "there is a physical difference between the white and black races which I believe will forever forbid the two races living together on terms of social and political equality."[26] The less tactful segments of the public were more blunt. A Dayton resident told a race relations investigator, "This is the way I class the nigger among the races: (1) the white man, (2) the Mongolian, (3) the Japanese, (4) the Chinese, (5) the dog, and last, the nigger."[27] Such comments were not surprising in view of the fact that one of the chief architects of "scientific" racism, Dr. Josiah C. Nott of Mobile, Alabama, liked to describe his field as "niggerology."[28]

The belief in racial hierarchy gave rise to another just as insidious. Race theorists, in asserting the fact of permanent and wide racial differences, implied as well that the differences led inevitably to racial incompatibility. At the time of the Civil War, when Fleet Walker had not yet reached his teens, the Negro, according to many white Americans, had already peaked culturally and only then through the good fortune of contact with whites. Having reached a plateau, Negroes, according to many whites, would become extinct once their purpose in America had been served. Further, all of this was seen as resulting from the free operation of "natural laws," a concept that would have great bearing on Walker's later views of human relations. Thus, many thought it to be in America's interest, North and South, to begin deportation and colonization of blacks. Even important Northerners like Ohio Congressman James A. Garfield confessed, "I would be glad if they could be colonized, sent to heaven, or got rid of in any decent way."[29] In Africa, the Negro would not be forced to contend with the superior Anglo-Saxon qualities of liberty, virtue, individual enterprise, resourcefulness, and practicality. There blacks could find cultural and geographical conditions more suited to their own inescapable racial traits – passivity, promiscuity, simple-mindedness, moral indifference – in short, those associated with the stereotypes of the slave plantation, and not coincidentally those most useful in tying blacks to the centuries-old portrayals of Africans as subhuman creatures of the jungle.

Words that would later spill out of Fleet Walker confirmed his intimate knowledge of and belief in the idea of irreversible trait distinctions that ran through his bloodstream. Moses and Caroline had given him his Negro blood, and maybe that was a great enough disadvantage for a child to bear in a society that had created racial lore powerful enough to force people of color to be mindful at every step of slavery, segregation, the human issues of equality and freedom, the scientific theories of race distinction, and the hopes for race progress. But his parents had also passed along to him their own measures of Caucasian blood. The hierarchical schemes of race theorists did not easily accommodate all the subtle hues that race mixing implied, but they found a way nonetheless to deal with aberrations like Fleet Walker.

According to nineteenth-century race theorists like Nathaniel Southgate Shaler, a Kentucky aristocrat with a position at Harvard's Lawrence Scientific School, the result of allowing white and black blood to mix was the creation of a "third something," a hybrid race contemptuously labeled "neither fish nor fowl" by some Southerners, and "yellow niggers" by others less courteous still.[30] Mulattos, according to the theorists, were like human mules, having no species identity of their own and no capacity for reproduction. Fleet Walker was such a "human mule."

By 1860 the nation's half-million mulattos, if considered black, constituted just thirteen percent of the total Negro population. If considered white, they were a statistically negligible segment of that population. And yet their presence was anything but negligible, eliciting instead disproportionate attention. It is strange that whites would regard the blood of the allegedly inferior Negro race as powerful enough to threaten the Anglo stock. If whites were actually superior, or were even convinced of their superiority, it would have made sense to regard race mixing as inconsequential for Caucasians and beneficial to the genetic makeup of Negroes.

There was, however, a powerful reason why whites dealt irrationally with explanations of mulatto status: the intolerable recognition that mulatto children were the visible evidence of sexual intercourse between the races. Sex between the races was a taboo that undermined white notions about racial purity and racial incompatibility. The economic necessity of colonial tobacco growers to control and eventually enslave their workforce had led to early prohibitions against interracial sex. In 1662 the Virginia legislature declared miscegenation a crime, with a fine twice that for other kinds of illicit sex. The same law also announced that the mulatto children of slave women would be slaves themselves. This broke the English tradition in which a child inherited the status of its father, but favored the building of a large slave force.[31]

Ironically, just as race theorists sought to attach the labels of *superior* and *inferior* to perceived race differences, the forced demand for separate racial sexual liaisons inevitably created comparisons between black and white sexuality that carried deep emotional meaning. A myth of black sexuality arose, magnified by lurid tales that seventeenth- and eighteenth-century Europeans and Americans told of Africans and their "giant penises, intercourse with apes, and assorted unspeakable (but much spoken of) transgressions against God and nature."[32] By the twentieth century, the idea of black sexual prowess had helped to establish a complementary myth of white sexual inadequacy that sentenced white males to a prison of their own making. It became the only American jail to which blacks held the keys.

By the midnineteenth century, the general wish of whites to dissociate from mulattos was evident and, to them, understandable. Still, mulattos presented a visible affront to the idea of race separation, and it became necessary for whites to rationalize the existence of these "new people" by constructing for them a special set of myths that could merge and accommodate the most pronounced and scientific tenets of their beliefs about white superiority and Negro inferiority.

To cast a suitably dim light on continued intimacy between whites and blacks, some race theorists warned that the Negro's position as a separate species, one that predated even Adam and Eve, made attempts to physically amalgamate with whites through intermarriage the targets for "catastrophic divine intervention." Others argued that the scientific laws that compelled species to seek their own survival explained not only white aversion to "hybridity," but also was a rational explanation for prejudice of color.[33] Nearly all agreed that mulattos were less prolific than either whites or Negroes and that the mixed stock that came from interspecies breeding would be prone to a diminishing capacity for reproduction for several generations and then to eventual extinction.

Whites devised other myths beyond that of eventual sterility as anchors for their perceptions of the mulatto soul. White Americans thought that mulattos were more physically attractive than blacks, but constitutionally weak, prone to debilitating diseases, and unable to endure the heat of a summer sun. They believed that mulattos were more intelligent than blacks, but also rather flighty, temperamental, and unwilling to endure hard physical labor. Mulattos had the negative Anglo-Saxon tendency toward tyranny, and the mulatto sons of white fathers – even as portrayed in *Uncle Tom's Cabin* – were thought to be particularly restive and resistant. Mulattos, according to whites, held themselves aloof from blacks, considering themselves superior. Tellingly, they always married light and never dark.[34]

While the prejudice of whites against mulattos was predictable, the less understandable and more subtle antagonism that blacks themselves evinced towards mulattos deepened the difficulty of living as a hybrid. Just after the turn of the century, the famous black leader, W. E. B. Du Bois, would assert that all Negroes lived in a spiritual bind, slaves to a double consciousness brought on by their African past and their American present. But Moses Fleetwood Walker and other mulattos knew decades before that the double identity could be more than a matter of spirit. They were the biological manifestations of an African-American cross, and it made them objects of mistrust among many dark-skinned Negroes.

While a great deal of intermarriage took place between free blacks and whites, mulattos were a symbolic reminder of the imposition of white masters on their slave women, couplings that stirred the greatest antagonism toward sex between the races. This problem, exacerbated by the belief of whites that black women were lascivious by nature, was a difficult one for white society. But it was just as discomfiting for blacks and contributed to a low regard for the slave mothers of mulatto children. Some blacks indicted these women as willing consorts of the slavemaster. For some mulattos, as with later figures like Malcolm X, their white features served as a reminder of former oppression and became a source of embarrassment, self-hatred, and seething resentment toward whites.

A brief window of tolerance, at least from blacks, opened for mulattos after the Civil War when many former slaves embraced the union of mulattos and blacks in the hope that the lighter-skinned hybrids would provide an avenue of social mobility into the white world for all people of color. It would not work out that way. Though blacks often hid their animosity toward mulattos from whites, this did not soften its sting. Being a mulatto, then – part white, part black – perched one atop the fence that separated the races. There was no right way to turn. A step either way brought a fall. It was a precarious condition, one that simply ran in the blood.

The Walkers' bloodlines imposed huge demands on the family members, suspending their identities between a fervid interest in their African heritage and their hopes for eventual social assimilation into the white world. Like many mulattos in the early years of Reconstruction, Moses W. Walker may have thought that as the country moved to a two-tier caste system, whites would absorb him, like other "third somethings," into the upper tier. Whether from this belief, from simple ambition, or from defiant anger, Moses W. drew the energy to escape some of the limitations of his color. In doing so he left another legacy to Fleet, one that told him that a man's identity could be altered through career choices.

Sometime between 1850 and 1860 Moses W. began to redefine himself. By 1860 he had moved the family about twenty miles northeast to Steubenville – and he had become a physician. Since the issue of admitting blacks to medical schools never arose before 1865, and because Ohio had, after 1833, repealed all laws pertaining to the practice of medicine, Moses almost certainly learned the trade through the common practice of apprenticeship, a method that usually entailed about three years of reading and interning.[35] White physicians were one of the first groups to publicly study the differences between blacks and whites in the nineteenth century, their observations contributing to white perceptions of Negroes as people prone to debilitating disease and poor health, sometimes the result of alleged moral and intellectual shortcomings. As the first black doctor in Steubenville, and one of the first in Ohio, Moses would have the daily opportunity to confront the reality of black health and, since his practice included delivering babies, the truth regarding mulatto sterility. His new position also gave him the opportunity to explore the distinctions of both color and class within the community.

When he moved to Steubenville's second ward, taking up residence with Caroline, the children, and Esther Eddy, an eighty-five year old Virginia-born woman, he left the guarded and unique race relations of Mount Pleasant for the more stratified life of a large manufacturing and coal mining town that was also the seat of Jefferson County.[36] He must have chosen his new home carefully, however, for Steubenville shared Mount Pleasant's reputation for racial tolerance. Republicans in the area had joined those all over northeast Ohio in clamoring for black suffrage as early as 1865. Town industry was not only integrated, but blacks actually controlled several of the skilled trade unions. Late in the century, when the nation's racial attitudes were growing noticeably uglier, black couples frequented Steubenville's Opera House without incident.[37] That may have been so, though whites still defined the barriers that limited contact between the town's races in certain social matters.

The education of the Walker children is uncertain. An 1872 history of Steubenville claimed that blacks that year, when Fleet was fifteen, were attending a "flourishing" black school at the corner of Third and South Streets, to which a legislative act had granted privileges corresponding to those of the white schools. Sometime thereafter, however, Steubenville integrated its schools, without complaint and in deference to the economic disadvantage of maintaining separate facilities. It likely did so shortly after 1872 because in 1910 both Fleet and Weldy were listed as alumni of Steubenville High School.[38]

Growing up in a place like Steubenville, caught between the inflexible demands for segregation that increasingly rolled up from the South after the War and the insistence of some Northerners for complete social equality, must have been much like being a mulatto. The tantalizing nearness of so many ideals may have actually increased the frustration that came when they were thwarted. As a young boy, Fleet Walker undoubtedly came to know, if not understand, that color still outweighed class. He was the son of the town's only black doctor, a profession lucrative enough to have brought his father a house worth $3,000 – six times the value of the family home in Mount Pleasant – and personal property worth $500, a small fortune at a time when a laborer in the state might earn $1.50 for twelve hours of work. A black newspaper estimated in 1890 that the value of property owned by Negroes in the United States amounted to an average of only $200 per family, a finding that would place the Walkers among the very well-off in the 1860s and 1870s.[39]

In 1870 the household not only supported five children, including twenty-five-year-old William (who claimed no occupation) and Weldy (born in 1860), but also Jennie Brown, a seventeen-year-old mulatto girl from Pennsylvania. Still, the Moses W. Walker family's move to a second Steubenville address, while placing them in an integrated neighborhood in the town's first ward, did not place them among the white elite. Rather, their neighbors included a glassblower, a schoolteacher, a coal miner, a teamster, a butcher, a tailor, and a carpenter. Moses must not have regarded his situation as totally satisfactory because by 1870 he had once more redefined himself, this time in a way that would allow him a more active role in black issues. Now fifty years old, Moses Walker was a minister of the Methodist Episcopal Church.[40]

While he had been too old to fight the Civil War in the Union's colored troops, Moses had found other ways to express his position on civil rights. He had made the Walker homes in towns that were stops on the Underground Railroad. His decisions to adopt two children and provide a home for several other blacks showed him to be a man sympathetic to the often involuntary mobility of the black population at midcentury. Certainly the obsession with equality that would grip Fleet and Weldy reflected their father's influence. But it was his work as a minister that would bring Moses nearer to the political power wielded by the church, still the institutional beacon of the black community, and associate him with the work of many black ministers who were challenging the dogma of white churches that preached racial passivity as the acceptance of God's will.

More consequential for Fleet, his father's newfound calling swept him to a place that would forever alter the direction of his life. In 1877 the church summoned Moses Walker to the leadership of one of the two Methodist Episcopal churches in Oberlin, Ohio. As pastor of the Second M. E. Church on South Water Street, he was charged with restoring order to a congregation divided by a wealthy member's assault charges against the previous minister. Walker's peacemaking was effective, though the church members recommended bickering after his departure for a new post in Jeffersonville, Indiana, in 1878.[41] By 1880 he was back in Steubenville – and with two adopted thirteen-year-olds, Mary and Charles.[42] But his stay in Oberlin, though brief, had been long enough to expose his namesake to the political interests of the church and to enroll him at the local college.

In January 1878 when Moses' church hosted a meeting to honor the fifteenth anniversary of the Emancipation Proclamation, the twenty-one-year-old Fleet Walker was secretary of the celebration committee. At this meeting Reverend Walker offered remarks relative to "the existing laws and customs proscribing the colored race." Several months previous, Fleet had been exposed to the prospects of black American colonization when the scheduled lecture for the church's dedication featured Bishop Gilbert Haven on "America in Africa."[43]

Whatever influence the church exerted paled next to that of Oberlin College. There Fleet Walker would meet both his future wives, rub elbows with those destined for leadership roles in the fight for Negro rights, trip on the roots of an unexpected career, and develop a detached intellectual bearing that would shield the deep emotions that divided his heart.

Oberlin was an exciting but dangerous place for a mulatto. Like Steubenville it may have led Fleet toward a false sense of possibilities. Located in Lorain County, thirty-two miles southwest of Cleveland, Oberlin was a small town carved out of a deep Ohio forest by pious transplanted easterners decades before the Civil War. Even more so than Mount Pleasant, it became a stronghold of abolitionism and a major link in the Underground Railroad. The men who founded Oberlin College in the early 1830s had done so in the wake of a dispute at Cincinnati's Lane Seminary that centered around the efforts of its students to grant Negroes an education and social equality. The 1834 decision of Oberlin's board of trustees to open the school to black students brought the college national attention, as did its insistence on admission for women.[44]

When Fleet Walker enrolled in Oberlin's preparatory program in 1877, at the age of twenty, the college's student body, comprising a Negro enrollment of five to ten percent, along with its provision for coed classroom experiences, reinforced its reputation as a liberal institution. In many ways, however, Oberlin was representative of the socially restrictive outlook that characterized most church-dominated schools in the nineteenth century. The catalog that governed students' lives was, at close reading, a menu for piety and grimness, one long diatribe against the pursuit of fun.

It began by telling candidates for admission that they first needed testimonials of good character and the "sufficient maturity and self-control to study profitably." It then detailed the routine of life for those lucky enough to gain admittance. Students were required to attend services at one of the town's six churches twice every Sunday, prayers at the college's chapel each evening, and prayers every morning with the family with which they boarded, religious ritual that would require little adjustment in Fleet Walker's schedule so long as he was under his father's roof.

Tobacco, alcohol, and secret societies were banned at Oberlin. Every recitation and exam was marked, every class absence recorded, and every barrier to progress or deportment subject to revelation to one's parents. No opposite-sex visits were permitted. Curfew for women never extended beyond 8:00 P.M., and every woman had to confess her successes and failures in observing regulations in a twice-monthly report signed by the matron of her boarding family. The final page of the catalog gave a last warning to the incorrigible to turn back. It noted that Oberlin "is remarkably free from the temptations and dangers often surrounding school life. There are no drinking saloons in town. But those who seek bad company will find it – or make it – anywhere, and the College does not offer itself as a reformatory for young people who are too wayward for home restraints."[45]

As at many colleges, the restraints that Oberlin imposed were usually far more daunting than those found at home, though Walker, as a twenty year old in his first year of preparatory work, may have found both places stifling. The preparatory program that readied him for admission examinations included English, algebra, plane geometry, ancient history, history of the United States, the science of government, and a slew of classical Greek and Latin compositions ranging from Virgil to Cicero to Homer.[46] In the fall of 1878, having passed the exams, he took his place among the class of 1882 in the classical and scientific course in the college's Department of Philosophy and the Arts. Just as important as admission was the fact that Walker's father had left town for his new church post.

Courses at Oberlin were graded on a six-point system, with 4.0 the lowest passing grade. Though he missed twenty-six classes, of the nine final grades posted for Walker in his first year, five were 6.0s, and he earned a 5.95 for his work in Horace and a 5.8 in the course on Lysias. His low mark was a 4.75 in "memorabilia," a course for which the general catalog offered no comment.

In his sophomore year, as internalized discipline lingering from a now distant family battled with the impetuosity of youth's first independence, Walker began to show evidence of a declining academic interest. He received 4.0 in two courses, and scores between 5.0 and 5.8 in seven others. His recorded absences rose from twenty-six the first year to forty-nine. Only two subjects captured his attention. In mechanics, a physics course that explored motions and forces, machines, and projectiles, Walker received a 6.0. He would later apply the knowledge of this course in emphatic ways. He also had a decided interest in rhetorical exercise, a class held weekly throughout the year. Consisting of reading essays and delivering original addresses, the class gave special prominence to extemporaneous speaking and discussion. Walker had a flair for the subject. He skipped the class relatively few times and of the five grades recorded for him, all were 6.0 Perhaps he knew that cultivating the skills of this class would one day serve him well, or perhaps he was merely enjoying the fruits of a gift he had brought with him to Oberlin. By his junior year, however, Walker had begun frequently to miss even the rhetorical exercise class; during the year he missed an astounding total of 123 classes. His grades continued to decline. In the final semester of 1881 he failed the course in "mental philosophy," and was failing at least two others.[47] Something had obviously become more interesting to him.

Actually, several things were exerting a stronger pull on him than the classroom, their collective wiles exploiting his inability to recognize limits. He was falling in love – not once, but twice and maybe thrice.

His first romantic choices revealed the extent to which the doctrine of race separation had dented both his psyche and Oberlin's claims to color blindness. Arabella Taylor, a pretty, light-skinned eighteen-year-old mulatto student from Xenia, Ohio, claimed one piece of his heart. Ednah Jane Mason, a pretty, light-skinned twenty-year-old mulatto student raised near Oberlin likely held another. The largest belonged to a game, a boy's fancy.

Baseball was an institution that had not only survived the Civil War but prospered from it, the relief it provided to bored and weary soldiers helping to plant the seeds for its phenomenal spread. During Fleet's childhood the game had been popular among Steubenville's boys,[48] and Walker was undoubtedly one of them. During his preparatory year in 1877 he caught and hit leadoff in a game in which the prep team beat the Oberlin town nine.[49] By his junior year his baseball fever had gained a grip that would hold him for most of the next decade. The short rope that tethered Oberlin's women students to virtue limited the time that Walker could spend at romance with Arabella or Ednah, but the college was handcuffed in its ability to control Walker's appetite for baseball.

His obsession with the game occurred during a transitional stage in the history of college athletics. Collegiate men had for decades been using interclass contests to dispel the gloom of study and propriety. The football matches between the classes at Harvard had become known as Bloody Monday, riotous occasions that administrators viewed as disruptive scars on the student body. Unable to contain them, however, college officials had begun in midcentury to regard physical outbursts as ineradicable expressions of male biological development. The best way to control them was not through deprivation, they believed, but by redirecting student energy toward constructive ends. Thus began a conscious recasting of athletic philosophy that combined elements from the British doctrine of amateurism, the belief in manly prowess, the need for healthy activity, and the growing quest for order to produce a rationale for sport as a character-building endeavor. College faculties and administrators increasingly believed that, controlled and pointed in proper directions, college athletes could become equal measures of Lancelot and Lincoln. Officials hoped that athletics, even among the untalented, could provide an outlet for the savage tendencies lurking in young males, draining off excessive energy that might otherwise be turned to marauding the refectory like so many juvenile Grendels. Thus sports could help foster the American educational goal of total student development.

Oberlin students took advantage of the faculty's weakening objections to their formerly rebellious pastimes by organizing sports clubs and beginning regular travel in the 1860s and 1870s to other colleges for matches. By 1880 this left the Oberlin faculty, like that at other colleges, in a bind. They were holding the tail of a tiger cub that would eventually grow into the terrorizing beast known as big-time intercollegiate sports. To let go would be to invite back the mayhem of the earlier unorganized class clashes and renege on their claims of the benefits of sport; to hold on meant to be helplessly dragged along by the unrelenting intent of students to spend as much time at sport as they desired. Oberlin's position was particularly resistant to a reconsideration of options.

Students had provided the labor needed to clear the trees, make the roads, and erect the buildings of Oberlin College in the 1830s, efforts that had fulfilled the new school's basic philosophy of "learning and labor."[50] Oberlin had mandated that both men and women devote several hours per day to manual chores, the principle objectives being "health, bodily, mental and moral, the student's support; and the formation of industrious and economical habits."[51] When the need for manual labor slackened several decades later, a system of gymnastics – formalized and somewhat static exercise – took its place. Gymnastic exercise shared with the manual labor system a belief in physical exertion as the means to an improved spirit and intellect. Its advocates, however, often expounded a negative attitude toward games and sports, not surprising since Oberlin had its share of contests reminiscent of Harvard's Bloody Monday. A football game at Oberlin in the 1860s was described as one in which "shirts sleeves would be torn off, suspenders would be burst and shins would be kicked rather more freely than the ball."[52] Still, administrators were hard-pressed to deny that sports, once brought to order, could benefit Oberlin students in the same way that manual labor and gymnastics had, inasmuch as all three shared an insistent belief in a mind-body nexus. Fleet Walker arrived at Oberlin at a time when the enthusiasm of the students for sports was testing the college's philosophic affirmation of physical exercise. The year that Walker enrolled in the preparatory program, gymnastic exercise became a requirement for all students. But by the time he left in 1881, Oberlin's students had successfully petitioned to establish an athletic association, the faculty had approved special construction of a baseball field, and gymnastic exercise had been excised from the required curriculum.[53]

Oberlin men had formed organized baseball clubs as early as 1865. Some, such as the Penfields – a club that included a "jet black" first baseman whose presence meant that Fleet Walker would at least not have to bear the title of "Oberlin's first black baseball player" – and the Resolutes, scheduled games away from campus; the latter, in fact, spent a summer traveling to neighboring towns for matches. Between 1869 and 1873 the faculty had banned competition against outside clubs, leaving interclass play as the primary alternative. By the fall of 1880 these interclass games had acquired a life so compelling that they were, according to the campus paper, luring "even the lean and wrinkled theologues," those students "with narrow chests and care-worn brows" to participate on class teams, thus providing the chance to "stir up the sluggish blood till it dances in warm red currents through your veins and you feel the heavy fogs breaking away from your clogged and over-worked brain."[54] The games became regular, intense, and so raucous that the college had to change the location of the playing field.[55]

It was an interclass game that fall that dedicated Oberlin's new baseball diamond and also gave Fleet Walker a first tiny taste of the public acclaim that the game might bring him. In the match between the junior and senior "first nines," Walker caught for the winning junior team and struck his legendary blow over Cabinet Hall. Both he and his batterymate, Harlan Burket, received special mention in the school paper, the *Oberlin Review*.

Burket, the son of a prominent Ohio attorney and future justice of the Ohio Supreme Court, had arrived at Oberlin nearly by accident. His first choice had been Wittenberg College, but his father feared the poor railroad connections to Springfield would only aggravate his son's anticipated homesickness. When the pair of Burkets pulled into the Oberlin station, however, a group of Oberlin students had just finished tarring and feathering an unpopular classmate, giving the father anxious second thoughts. "I don't know, Harl," he told his son, "it looks as if you are going to get into a tough bunch here at Oberlin." From the college escapades later recalled in Burket's diary, it is likely that other parents would have had greater reason to fear their children's associations with him. He never wanted for ways to fill his time. Nearly all took a backseat to baseball.[56]

In his first week at Oberlin, Burket encountered a student named Bessey (three students had this surname at that time), who used a green grape to show Burket how friction, grip, and release could be used to make a thrown object curve. After a winter of practicing with snowballs, Burket debuted in the spring of 1881 as the only "curved pitcher" in college, and one of only three in the state. Some college professors maintained that Burket was tossing nothing more than an optical illusion, but the young pitcher knew that his ability to bend a ball around the middle of three posts was real enough.[57] He also knew that it took a talented catcher to work effectively with him, a fact that would cause him to renew ties with Fleet Walker several times in the years ahead.

In 1881, Oberlin's faculty reversed their ban on games against teams from off campus. In fact, they approved formation of an athletic association for the express purpose of bringing in outside competition. It was exposure to this competition that would lure Walker away from Oberlin. The 1881 Oberlin baseball club became the school's first varsity intercollegiate team. It included Burket, Walker, and Fleet's younger brother, Weldy, who had enrolled at Oberlin as a member of the class of 1885.

The team played only five games, three of which were little more than practice, but they were enough to convince the Walkers to become pioneers in the practice of transferring colleges in search of a better fit for their athletic ambitions and talents. After homering, doubling twice, and singling in a game against a team of locals, Fleet also drew attention in a 4–0 victory over Michigan's Hudson College and a season-ending 9–2 win against the University of Michigan. According to Burket the finale inspired Michigan to coax Walker and teammate Arthur Packard to play the following season in Ann Arbor.[58] Weldy, in a role that would become common over the next thirty years, decided to tag along in Fleet's new venture.

By century's end, talented collegians would be routinely switching allegiances – sometimes weekly, sometimes under assumed names – in defiance of growing conference athletic rules that were also struggling to contain the new phenomena of recruiting, training tables, extensive travel, professional coaches, and competitive excess that was leading to injury and death in football. In 1881, however, eligibility was a trifling matter. In fact, Burket was called back to Oberlin to pitch several times after his graduation, the last in 1885 – two years after he had pitched for a high-level professional team. In 1881, then, the Walkers' decision to transfer drew little notice. In Fleet's case, it did, however, produce the first questions about his character.

For three years, Walker had shared the Oberlin campus with the likes of Mary Church Terrell, George Herbert Mead, Henry Churchill King, and Ida Gibbs Hunt, students who would go on to make considerable marks in the intellectual world.[59] Perhaps his success as Oberlin's catcher and the minor celebrity it brought him convinced Walker that he had found an avenue of achievement to rival that of Mead and the others. Though Burket thought "Harry" King was the strongest all-around man ever to graduate from Oberlin,[60] when King became Oberlin's president in 1903, his inaugural address contained remarks about college athletes that seemed swollen with envy and that might well have sprung from his remembrance of the special acclaim that baseball had brought to classmates during his undergraduate years, and from the later notoriety

Walker found in the game. Sports contributed to sanity and health, King claimed, but they were not merely for "a small number of specially athletic men." Rather, they had their greatest value "not as serious business or money-making enterprises, but simply as *play*."[61] Had Fleet Walker, in deciding to transfer to Michigan, lost sight of the play aspect? Had contact with baseball instilled character, or had his talent aggravated in him an attitude that King and other critics of college sport found just as common as character – one of arrogance, impunity, and elitism? Walker's application for admission to Michigan to begin baseball and law school in the spring of 1882 brought to light an unresolved incident at Oberlin and at least a partial answer.

In March, Michigan's president, James Angell, wrote to his Oberlin counterpart, James Harris Fairchild, for an opinion of Fleet Walker's general character. Walker's admission to Michigan had been jeopardized when he appeared there with papers from Oberlin "representing that he at one time did not state the exact facts or did not wholly keep his promise respecting his preparation for a certain examination." There is nothing more to explain the possible transgression and it is impossible to know what it entailed. The incident brought to attention, however, two other notes that shed light on Walker and the nascent power of college sport. One was among the papers Walker had carried with him to Michigan. It was from Charles Churchill, an Oberlin instructor who had taught mechanics to Walker, and it seemed to Angell to "extenuate very largely" Walker's offense.[62] A second letter in defense of Walker, this one from teammate Arthur Packard, pleaded with Fairchild:

> When Mr. Walker came here he thoroughly meant to go to work in earnest. After some difficulty he was finally admitted to examinations and had passed nearly all of them when Pres. Angell said that on account of a letter he had received from Oberlin his examinations should be stopped . . . This makes it very hard on Walker . . . He is almost hopeless and thoroughly downhearted . . . This affair has had a very deep effect on Mr. Walker and I know he will be very grateful if you will do something for him.[63]

Doing something for Walker would also be doing something for Packard and the Michigan baseball team, and Packard's athletic self-interest had a persuasive force behind it. His father was Civil War General and United States Congressman Jasper Packard, so the letter was not, as it appeared, merely the impotent plea of a fellow student. Walker played at Michigan that spring, so the matter was settled in his favor. Still, the tone of Packard's letter hints at Walker's sense of drama and a belief in the power of words, demeanor, and maybe athletic celebrity to extract oneself from adversarial situations. Regardless of how tight the spot and how deep the despair had appeared or been made to appear, even Walker had no way of knowing how crucial the admissions decision was. For at nearly the same time that the presidential letters were being exchanged, Fleet and Arabella Taylor had found a way to escape Oberlin's tight rein on student romance long enough for "Bella" to become pregnant.

Moses Fleetwood Walker departed for Michigan after that summer for a number of reasons: to pursue the study of law, an occupation that would financially reward his rhetorical flair and the ability to argue either side of an issue; to avoid whatever stigma he and Bella might suffer by remaining at Oberlin; and maybe just to fulfill a youthful desire for new experiences. Undoubtedly, he went primarily to play baseball. Ten years later James Fairchild's published remarks seemed aimed at Fleet and Weldy Walker, Harlan Burket, Arthur Packard, and other collegians who turned campuses into playgrounds. Perhaps the former college president recalled them all and Fleet's Michigan application when he wrote, "It is not established that the fullest muscular development, or the most perfect exhibition of the animal man, is most favorable to efficiency or power. It is by no means clear that muscle is sometimes not cultivated at the expense of the brain, and animal strength at the sacrifice of nervous energy and power." He continued in a way that foreshadowed the words of Harry King: "It is at least questionable whether he who makes a gymnast of himself is not sacrificing the higher to the lower nature, and whether, in the end, he is not the loser, even in the domain of power and achievement."[64]

Supporters of college sport have over the decades answered critics with some elaborate rationales. Athletes have seldom responded – they have not, after all, been the ones making exaggerated claims about character building. The rhetorician in young Fleet Walker could have undoubtedly strung together some lofty words to counter Fairchild's sentiment. But the best answer, the only wholly satisfactory one, lay in the secrets that muscles whisper only to the athletically gifted. Ironically, hitting would not distinguish Walker's approaching baseball career, but the body never forgets even the infrequent moments when bat meets ball perfectly, the electric currents coursing outward from the arms to galvanize the entire body. It is perhaps the sweetest of all athletic experiences. As the first ball disappeared over Cabinet Hall in October 1880, it may have been this ecstasy, forever encoded in his muscles, that began to carry Fleet Walker further from the classroom and ever nearer to a career dedicated to the pursuit of recalling the ecstasy over and over.

Down what path would the pursuit lead Fleet Walker? How far would the development of animal strength and power take him? How close would it bring him to consorting with the lower nature? Would he sacrifice the benefits of a cultivated mind only to become a loser?

In pursuing an answer, Walker would have the company of brother Weldy and the unwed and pregnant eighteen-year-old Bella Taylor. Ednah Mason remained at Oberlin; she would graduate in 1884. Other companions, new and old, though less visible, served as millstones to be carried on the journey: the name of his father and that of a biblical savior; the light color and mixed blood that put one foot on the doorstep of the white world and one on the plantation's doorsill; the issue-heavy legacy of Moses W., doctor and minister; and the mix of handsome face, winsome rhetoric, and athletic grace that would spell stardom for a select few in his generation. And maybe something or someone else, one more agent of division.

The censuses taken in the nineteenth century can be indispensable guides to family pasts, but also a bit like torn treasure maps that lead only to the brink of irrecoverable riches. This was never truer than in the case of the Walkers, whose census entries hint that Fleet Walker might have been a divided man from the moment of his conception. When the census taker left the Walker home in Steubenville's second ward in 1860, he had recorded more than one new child in the Walker family. Right below the entry for the three-year-old Moses Fleetwood Walker was the name of yet another three-year-old, Lizzie Walker. By 1870 she, along with Cadwallader, was gone from the family register.[65] Mortality schedules cannot track her disappearance. Given the nature of extended families in the nineteenth century and the need to shelter fugitive slaves, Lizzie Walker may have shared only a home with Fleet Walker. But she took her name from one of Caroline's sisters, and so it is plausible that she had shared Caroline's womb with Fleet. Modern psychology and ancient mythologies are rich with the lore of twins as complementary but opposite pieces of a whole, each incomplete without the other. Whether Fleet's Oberlin classes brought him to a consideration of classical twins like Castor and Pollux and the alternately rising and setting aspects of the Gemini constellation, the circumstances of his birth may have brought the lessons to him firsthand. Perhaps Lizzie's early departure had left him too much to carry – twin ambitions, a family's sense of loss, and all the demons that haunt a human with the specter of a life unlived. Maybe that is why, also, he invested the next decade of his life in living a game of youthful flight.

. . . .

Louisville 5; Toledo 1.

Those are the magic figures

that tell the story, and 'twas

all on account of a coon.

Louisville Commercial,

2 May 1884

INTO THE FIRE

When Moses Fleetwood Walker led Oberlin against Michigan in front of a capacity crowd in June 1881, the triumph could not have seemed more complete. The weather was bright, the collegial atmosphere just right, the victory resounding, the glory intoxicating. The *Oberlin Review* enshrined Walker's heroics in print. His play elicited Michigan's flattering entreaties, and his surrender to them meant he could enroll in law school and pursue a career matched to his gifts of persuasion and argument. The day also revealed another aspect of baseball that would intensify Walker's interest in the sport.

The Oberlin team had spent the morning before the game making a lobster trap of the playing field, using canvas, wood, and policemen to seal off the grounds from those who might otherwise not pay. When six hundred spectators funneled in with their quarters and half-dollars,[1] it must have been clear to Walker that baseball had become irresistible bait to the American public. How could he have known that the trap was set for him? Spectators would go free at the end of a game, but for the next nine years baseball would hold Walker captive, feeding him an addictive mix of money, excitement, and notoriety to dull the effects of rancor, futility, injury, and, of course, division. The nature of this new profession – and of those who worked at it, those who watched it, and those who wrote about it – would combine with the increasingly divisive nature of race relations to pull at the threads holding together this educated, charming, handsome, but volatile man.

The first tug was sudden and hard. Just two months after the triumph against Michigan, Walker got a glimpse at his future in a place that was light-years from the insularity of Oberlin. Most of the blacks who sent their children to Oberlin were assimilationist in their approach to the race question, preferring to believe that the country's future lay in integration rather than separation. Oberlin College, in fact, may have been freer of prejudice than any other white institution in the nation.[2] For the mulatto Walker, it may have offered a haven where the implications of his mixed blood were temporarily suspended. It was, nonetheless, a place that held out a possibility for social equality that was never quite fulfilled. Shortly after Fleet and Bella left, some white students began complaining about the custom of interracial seating during meals, protests that evolved over the next two decades into de facto segregation on campus. But if Oberlin was an imperfect place, Fleet Walker, in his inclination and insistence on becoming part of the national game, was heading toward more combustible and dangerous locales. In August 1881 Walker was paid to play catcher in a game for the White Sewing Machine Company, of Cleveland, a team that claimed several future major leaguers. He had apparently done so before without incident, but this game was in Louisville, Kentucky, and it would reveal to Walker the drawbacks to an affair with professional baseball.

On the morning of the game, he was turned away from breakfast at Louisville's Saint Cloud Hotel. Though it would be another half-decade before any segregationist Jim Crow laws appeared in the statutes of a Southern state, the rejection was consistent with the South's post–Civil War resolve to separate the races. Notorious Black Codes had briefly and unevenly tried to proscribe race mixing on Southern railroads, in schools, and in public places. The details of separate arrangements were not spelled out, however. Following repeal of the codes, custom served to reinforce their intentions. Discrimination was enforced through the withdrawal of white patronage and bolstered by the complicity of Negroes, who seldom breached the arrangements.[3] Eventually, when the refusals became commonplace in the years afterward, Fleet Walker refused to bow quietly to custom, but on this first trip into the South, he offered no reprisals.

When Walker arrived at the field for pregame practice, the alienation escalated as managers and some of the players of the Louisville Eclipse club objected to his presence. Though Walker was their regular catcher, Cleveland yielded to the objections and began the game without him.

After one inning, his substitute behind the plate claimed his hands were so badly bruised that he could not continue, and the crowd of two to three thousand people began calling "in good nature for the 'nigger.'" A vice president of the Louisville club attempted to persuade Walker to come onto the field. His entreaties were met with reluctance. When Walker moved nearer, the crowd cheered. Still Walker hesitated. Finally, in a defining moment that mixed courage with imprudence, the young catcher threw off his coat and vest, stepped onto the diamond, and, as the game waited, began to warm up in a tense moment of public isolation. After he had made several "brilliant throws and fine catches," two Louisville players undermined their vice president's invitation by stalking off to the clubhouse. The game could not proceed until Cleveland's third baseman finally volunteered to go behind the plate. Walker never entered the game, and Louisville beat the Whites, 6–3.

The episode imparted to Walker these certainties: if he played baseball, his color was going to lead to some bad moments and some humiliation; but it was also going to be a badge of distinction and a guarantee of the spotlight's focus. A mulatto was entertainment, a magnet to a crowd.

The *Louisville Courier-Journal* account also made clear that a mulatto baseball player made an excellent foil for public examination of the race question. The commercial presses in cities would not be so uncritical as the *Oberlin Review* had been – nor as color-blind. From now on, for good or bad, Fleet would seldom if ever find himself identified as simply "Walker." Now adjectives – North and South, benign and malicious – would appear in front of "Walker," affixed as if they were his first name: *colored, coon, brunette, Negro, dusky, mulatto, Spanish.* Sometimes he would simply become an object, such as the "negro catcher." In Louisville he was "the quadroon." Thus, assessments of his performance nearly always begged association with the question of color. The *Courier-Journal* observed that "no rules provide for the rejection of 'race, color or previous condition of servitude.' The crowd was anxious to see Walker play, and there was no social question concerned." By managing to bring up race, color, and slavery, the paper insured, of course, that there was in fact a vital social question concerned.[4]

The matter-of-fact way in which the *Louisville Courier-Journal* reported the game revealed the slippery way in which newspapers appeared to deplore racism while winking at it. The coverage strongly criticized the local club, advocated that Cleveland sue for damages, and declared that Walker had "earned the reputation of being the best amateur catcher in the Union." Still, the mention of the "good-natured" call for the "nigger" was a journalist's device that literally whitewashed the situation's implicit menace. In 1881 a crowd of several thousand was a large one, and their behavior could turn unmanageable. Unlike the modern era, in which wire and concrete barriers, distance, and the aura of sacred space combine to assist officials in protecting players, in the 1880s ropes and rickety wooden bleachers failed to restrain fans who hemmed the playing field and blurred the boundaries between audience and performer. It was an era that lent real malice to the cry, "Kill the umpire," and "good nature" just shielded malevolent intent behind an oily grin.

Playing for Michigan the following spring brought Walker a temporary return to more accepting and comfortable surroundings. Though the prior year's Ann Arbor team had sworn off drinking and smoking during their trip to Oberlin, they had not fared well there or elsewhere. The team had been weakest behind the plate, even though at times they had gone so far as to hire their catchers. The recruitment of Walker, who would be both a student and a player the campus newspaper promised would "give entire satisfaction," was vital. During the winter, team aspirants practiced daily in the gymnasium and raised money for new uniforms and field care, inspiring hopes that 1882 would be a better year.[5] In April the former Oberlin battery of Packard and Walker combined talents in a game against Oberlin's sophomore team. Walker homered in his new team's victory.[6] By the end of May, Michigan had won its first six games. Walker, hitting second, reprised his legendary Oberlin home run in a game against Madison (Wisconsin). With two outs, two strikes, and two on base, he "struck the ball square in the face for the most beautiful home run seen on the grounds this year," and then crossed home plate to "tumultuous applause." As always, however, it was his catching that earned Walker the most plaudits and the college paper's appellation as "the wonder." In a 20–3 victory, for example, Walker had three passed balls while his Northwestern counterpart had ten.[7] Michigan won ten of its thirteen games in 1882. In its games against opponents in the Western College League, Fleet hit .308, singling eight times in twenty-six at bats.[8]

That July he insured the legitimacy of his unborn child by marrying Bella Taylor in Hudson, Michigan, not far from the Ohio line. The marriage certificate listed her residence as nearby Hillsdale, and later documents claimed her as a graduate of Hillsdale College.[9] The college has no record that Bella ever attended a class there, however. Further, the school is nearly seventy miles from Ann Arbor, which would have required the newlyweds to live apart. She and Fleet did, in fact, live apart that summer, but it was Fleet's doing. He had scarcely been married for a month when he left Michigan for New Castle, Pennsylvania, and his first extended hitch in professional baseball.

A baseball hotbed some fifty-five miles north of Pittsburgh, New Castle was an auspicious town for a baseball debut. In 1882 two teams vied for the attention and dollars of the New Castle townsfolk: the Blue Stockings and the newly formed Neshannocks, named for the town's river that was itself named after the Indian word for black potato.[10] The "Nocks" gained the upper hand when they offered enough money to secure ex-Oberlin pitcher Harlan Burket for the summer. In mid-July – though another ex-Oberlin teammate, Ed Burwell, seemed to be handling Burket adequately – rumors began appearing in the local paper that "a gentleman named Walker, one of the best catchers in the country," would be arriving to support Burket. The day before he was to alight in New Castle, the paper called Walker "undoubtedly the best amateur ball player in the country," and "a gentleman in every sense of the word, both on the ball field and off."[11] Ironically, it was Burwell who may have given rise to these glowing pronouncements. As late as 1934 he told a former classmate that Walker was "the finest catcher he had ever seen play."[12] A further curiosity is that while Burket, in his brief account of his baseball experiences, later wrote of his friend Burwell's position with the Nocks, he scarcely mentioned Walker's company, either at Oberlin or New Castle. Perhaps a clue to Burket's snub is found in the delight he took as an Oberlin student in helping to stage a minstrel show.[13] Though he may not have considered Walker his social equal, his wish to have his college batterymate in New Castle acknowledged that the catcher's addition would add to the Neshannocks' growing reputation as one of the nation's strongest nine.[14]

In light of the dollars that some of New Castle's "monied sporting men" had spent to assemble the Neshannocks, the term *amateur* as applied to Burket and Walker was a matter of convenience, one meant to convey the more genteel spirit of play thought to reside within collegians. In light of the postwar uneasiness wedging the black and white populations apart, it was a matter of good sense to neglect to mention Walker's race, stressing instead his character. New Castle, of all Walker's professional bases, was the only town where the local press never made mention of his color, likely a circumstance of politics or good fortune. This did not mean, however, that the New Castle press or residents were color-blind. They were as aware of race and its implications as any other Americans.

In the months surrounding Walker's stay in New Castle, the *Daily City News* had run stories that suggested the threat to order that the irrational, primitive emotions of blacks, particularly women, posed. A "bad colored girl" had drawn editorial reprimand for the ruin of her many black and white suitors, young men who, without her seductions, would have made "good and useful citizens."[15] In August, just before Fleet Walker began catching for the Nocks, the paper printed a lengthy innuendo about the activities of a local black Baptist minister. In doing so, nearly every tenet of perceived race difference – and fear – found expression in prose that dripped with sensual imagery:

> As the moon controls the tides of the ocean so does the god of day influence and shape the actions of the dusky descendants of Ham. When Old Sol is farthest from the earth they lie in peace beside the nearest stove, but when the red hot rays shot forth on July days penetrate their places of retreat they awake from their slumber, strop the testive razor, and with eyeballs protruding several inches out upon their cheek bones, and scalding steam issuing from every pore of their perspiring frames which act as safety valves for the seething hearts within, they hie them hence to Hayti.

The article went on to describe the jealous dispositions of black men and their widespread suspicion of the fidelity of their wives. A validating characterization of black women as Amazons willing to do physical battle for the attentions of the "Adonis-like form" of their reverend minister followed.[16]

It was impossible to know at that moment in what ways these beliefs were finding their way into Fleet Walker's psyche. Did his mind, like that of whites, make a distinction between his new wife – so light as to be often mistaken for white – and the darker-skinned women being castigated as Amazons? Had he intentionally sought, as mulatto mythology demanded, a mate lighter than himself?

It is just as difficult to know in what ways the indirect slights of racial intolerance were creating division in a man who was not only conversant with the foundations of white cultural elitism, but given as well to taking part in them. If such matters were beginning to force Fleet into an untenable position between blacks and whites in 1882, he had Weldy along as ally and buffer. His brother had joined him to play a handful of games at second base for the Nocks. Whether their brief stay provided an antidote to Fleet's unsettling Louisville experience, or a more subtle complement to it, it did allow them their first competition against a National League team.

New Castle native Charlie Bennett, who had played for an earlier incarnation of the Neshannocks, was in the fourth year of a fifteen-year major league career when he brought his Detroit team to his hometown for an 1882 exhibition with the Nocks. In a nine-inning game played in one hour and fifteen minutes (Detroit had a train to catch and did little to risk the possibility of missing it), the two catchers, Bennett and Walker, each went one-for-four and committed two errors. Though Detroit beat Burket, 5–1, the game did nothing to dissuade the New Castle battery from a belief in the opportunities of professional baseball. The game drew so many New Castle spectators that some were forced to swarm through the surrounding trees for vantage points. They filled them until the branches sagged nearly to the ground.[17]

Though Walker had "surprised the natives as well as members of the Nocks" with "his brilliant work behind the bat," when he and Weldy left New Castle in early September, the local papers issued nary a good-bye. The team disbanded shortly thereafter, but the town's fans anticipated that the Oberlin trio of Burket, Burwell, and Walker would all return for the 1883 season.[18] For the Walkers the end of this season meant a return to college studies to wait for the start of the next.

Fleet resumed his law studies at Michigan. Weldy joined him in Ann Arbor in the fall of 1882, electing to try to follow his father's footsteps into medicine by enrolling in Michigan's homeopathic medical school. Homeopathy, a theoretical approach that favored intimate doctor-patient relationships and minute doses of medicines that replicated a disease's symptoms, had been popular in antebellum America, but in the 1880s Michigan was one of a small number of colleges still offering homeopathic coursework.[19] Weldy pursued the degree for two years. Following in Fleet's wake, he even became Michigan's catcher for several games in the spring of 1884. His medical career never came to fruition, however, his failure to graduate again echoing the actions of his older brother. Fleet intermittently pursued a legal career during the early eighties, at one point interning in the law offices of two white Steubenville attorneys, A. C. Lewis and John McClave, but even though the Michigan program required just two nine-month periods of classwork, he never finished it.[20] As had been the case at Oberlin, university classes proved no match for baseball. Both Walker brothers were intent on answering the calls of professional baseball, a decision made just as the game's determination to become the national pastime was about to intersect with the nation's determination to separate its white and colored citizens.

There is scarcely a baseball historian alive who has not recounted Mark Twain's observation that baseball was the very symbol of the struggle of the "raging, tearing, booming nineteenth century"[21] and noted its application to an industrializing, urbanizing America. Few have stopped to ponder the negative, sometimes literal implications that raging, tearing, and booming had for a society threatening to be forever divided over matters of color and conscience. Whatever its later nostalgic appeal, professional baseball in the 1880s was bent on giving assistance to the increasingly popular sentiment among whites for a more formal division of the white and black populations into two social castes. This determination seemed misguided in light of the obvious contradiction that it created for national ideals like democracy. But baseball's tendency toward segregation, and Fleet Walker's opposition to it, were profound in a more specific, crucial, yet nearly unspoken way.

Of all the different arenas in which to seek equality and success – political, economic, social, intellectual – baseball was the only one that offered to Fleet Walker not only an interregional, highly visible platform, but also an irrefutable, competitive disproving ground for fiercely held racial beliefs that were embedded in anatomy and physiology – that presumed blacks to be an inferior race because of their physical attributes. In drawing out once more the white fears of black physical prowess, professional baseball opened to Walker a broad avenue for pressing the case for racial equality. By playing baseball, he would become a traveling poster for Negro aspirations, one held up almost daily in the faces of white Americans, as in this 1883 newspaper announcement:

> NOTES
> Game to-day at 3:30
> Only one game this week
> Secure your season tickets at once
> See Walker, the great colored catcher[22]

Paradoxically, while race "scientists" of the late nineteenth century drew elaborate analogies between the biological constitution of apes and Negroes, most of their concerns led back to the brain, the skull, and the intelligence levels of blacks as compared to whites. Though side-by-side drawings of blacks and gorillas insinuated a savage and barbaric black population, scarcely ever were direct conclusions drawn about the physical capacities of blacks relative to whites. To admit the possibility of a physical power lurking within the black population was to invite unsettling images of Negro retribution reminiscent of Nat Turner and earlier slave rebellions – images too frightening to acknowledge. Myths of black indolence and docility produced more soothing stereotypes.

As long as whites were able to restrict racial comparisons to intelligence and character, they were willing to entertain and even embrace the idea of competition with blacks. In fact, a good many pitied the stereotyped passive Negro who had been turned loose by the Civil

War only to flounder in a free-market struggle against the aggressive and superior competitive nature believed to be carried in Anglo-Saxon genes. Many whites interpreted the meaning of Darwin in a free, competitive society in a manner so wishful that they looked anxiously to census figures in 1880 and later for confirmation that the black population might be declining, bearing out earlier predictions that an emancipated Negro race would become an extinct one. But even while the arguments for race difference focused on intellectual and moral capacities, race theorists were unable to detach them from their biological, physical foundations. This inability left white Americans who were inclined to favor race separation on anything more than emotional grounds in an untenable position when faced with the question of black physicality. They had several options. They could remain convinced of black docility even in the face of cases of black bravery exhibited in the Underground Railroad and the Civil War. They could go beyond mere ideas of docility and mistake black morbidity and mortality rates as evidence of black physical degeneracy, or they could, whenever possible, ignore the matter altogether. This last would be hard to do with someone like Fleet Walker running around American baseball diamonds and turning up as a cause célèbre in American newspapers.

Of course, it would not be easy to be that cause célèbre. The 1880s would offer a limited and severe test to a Negro brazen enough to become a public exhibit. To fly in the face of wishful white belief in a myth of black incapability, Fleet Walker would have to play well while simultaneously soothing white fears. This would require him to balance two opposing personal traits. He would have to exhibit his specialness, but with comportment. His flair for the dramatic, his showman's soul could not exceed his ability to check a darker side that would be constantly goaded by racial tensions. But Moses Fleetwood Walker was no ordinary man, and in the 1880s he was no ordinary baseball player.

By the reckoning of the census, and perhaps by his own as well, Fleet Walker was not yet a Negro at all. He was still a mulatto. Photographs indicate that he was noticeably lighter and more "white-featured" than brother Weldy. As always, this appearance would be a double-edged sword. To some blacks and whites, his lightness would translate to ambiguity, mistrust, and suspicion. To some, it would be a sign of status, but one that could easily turn to envy and hostility. And even if it did help grease his entrance into professional ball, it could just as easily backfire on him. If white beliefs about mulattos held true, Fleet Walker would never withstand the grueling schedule of a summer of play. The U.S. Sanitary Commission's wartime study had unequivocally concluded that mulattos had "inferior vitality," that physiologically they were inferior to the original stock of both blacks and whites. They were unfit for the rigors of competitive life.[23] In fact, if some neurologists were correct in asserting that electrical signals in the body ran in opposite directions in blacks and whites,[24] mulattos would literally have their wires crossed. Fleet Walker had already given the lie to one point of mulatto mythology when Bella gave birth to Cleodolinda Dewers Walker in December 1882. By decade's end the couple had added two sons, Thomas Fleetwood (1884) and George Wise (1886), to the cumulative argument the Walkers offered against the alleged sterility of mulattos. Further, Fleet Walker was not part of society's mudsill. He was educated, erudite, possessed of social grace and the good sense to display humility. It may be that his start in baseball, his chance to display physical prowess, came in part because of his character and education.

Professional baseball was not the usual career choice for a collegian in the 1880s. While colleges were busy exploiting the alleged nobility of an amateur code to dampen the ungentlemanly behavior associated with excessive student interest in athletics, professional baseball was struggling to overcome a sour public reputation woven in the 1870s of rowdyism, gambling, cheating, drinking, disorder, and chaos. It is unlikely, then, that professional baseball in the early 1880s, as it strove to overcome its troubles, would have tolerated a rowdy mulatto when there were already plenty of white hooligans to go around. Walker the collegian gave no indications that behavior would be a problem. Rather, the paradox was that an apparently cultured young man, exposed to the manners of the socially elite, would so readily associate with such a base profession. In retrospect, it is clear that neither Walker's temperament nor the possibilities for social fulfillment in other professions were what they seemed. Whether the lure of playing baseball for money was as seductive to young men in 1880 as it would become a century later, Walker must have heard it as a siren's call. He answered.

Though both Michigan and New Castle were probably expecting his return in 1883, Walker found the door to money and recognition opened wider elsewhere. William Voltz, a former *Cleveland Plain Dealer* sportswriter, had seen Walker and Burket play for Oberlin. When Voltz became manager of the Toledo club in the Northwestern League, he signed Walker to catch, reuniting him again with Burket, the team's first signee. Burket later recalled that 1883, owing to a three-day snowstorm in late May and a killing frost in early autumn, became known as "the year without a summer." It was not so for Fleet Walker. While Burket proved not fast enough, by his own admission, to hold his own in the Northwestern League,[25] the summer of 1883 was the liftoff phase for the professional career of his college catcher.

While he would in the course of his career occasionally play in the outfield, Walker would continue primarily as a catcher, a circumstance that would carry greater meaning amid the everyday rigors of high-level play. The position was a vital one, and its demands added another layer of Darwinian stress to Walker's life. In addition to leaving him in close proximity to the fans who crowded the playing field, it made him a central player in a game that was just beginning to grope its way toward the geometric and psychic perfection that would send its twentieth-century fans into nostalgic rapture.

Pitchers in the 1880s discarded underhand tosses, beginning first to throw sidearm, and then overhand, from fifty feet away. They began their romance with breaking balls and other whimsically named trick pitches like the "wave" ball. Deceptive deliveries became individual trademarks. One of Toledo's pitchers concocted a delivery that challenged the descriptive capabilities of the *Sporting Life* correspondent who wrote, "he turns his back to the umpire with a get-the-be-hind-me-Satan sort of an air, dances a double shuffle on the four corners of the box, and for want of something else to do, pitches."[26] Added to the absence of the protective armor that have become known as the tools of ignorance, the deliveries made catching a dangerous, nascent science. Catchers sometimes stood well back of the plate, which in the 1880s was often made of marble, to protect their unpadded hands. With runners on base, however, or in third-strike situations that required the ball to be caught on the fly, they had to move closer to the batter. The result was that runners ran wild as boxscores swelled with catchers' errors and passed balls. Further, sportswriters focused on the defensive performances of catchers, often portraying them as the pivotal elements in a victory or loss. The statistical ambiguities and the close scrutiny of the press made it difficult to sort out the relative skills of catchers. A strong arm like Walker's could be an asset one day, an untamed menace the next.

Certainly, there could have been no better position for disproving the myth of mulatto physical weakness or reluctance. In addition to playing in the hot flannel uniforms of the day, catchers spent a lot of time nursing broken and swollen fingers, bruised and battered bodies. A timid or frail man would not survive behind the plate. In the first week of the Toledo Blue Stockings' 1883 season, a foul ball hit Walker so hard that it bent the wires of his mask, raised a lump over his right eye, and left him dazed. He stayed in the game. A fortnight later he broke his thumb in the first of a three game series. According to Burket, when Walker "split" his hand he "crippled the team to such an extent" that they lost all three games.[27] Years later, John Robinson, an Oberlin resident, said that Walker would pass through town during his baseball days, stopping to share tips with the town's children, including one on how to hold the hand "to prevent broken fingers."[28] Obviously aware, then, of the need for self-protection, Walker nonetheless played on at a position whose fraternity regarded swollen, painful hands as a badge of manliness. The mask was the only equipment that he used regularly. Occasionally, according to a Toledo batboy, Walker wore ordinary lambskin gloves with the fingers slit and slightly padded in the palm; more often he caught barehanded. The batboy was only ten at the time. His remembrance decades later eulogized Walker: "I have seen him with his fingers split open and bleeding, but he would go right on catching. He had more nerve and grit than anybody I have ever seen."[29] While opposing catchers, including all three of Peoria's, limped weakly into the closing weeks of the season, Walker was still catching, "with few errors and without wincing."[30]

Nerve and grit explained part of Fleet Walker's persistent presence in Toledo's 1883 lineup. No doubt money also helped to soothe his many aches and pains. Unless Walker had a unique contract with Toledo, his income, like that of all ballplayers, was subject to the principle of payment only for services rendered. Sick, injured, or temporarily ineffective players received no pay. Salaries were large enough to induce players to endure fierce conditions to remain "affluent slaves."[31] At a time when laborers were earning ten dollars per week, some professional baseball players were making about two thousand dollars for a half-year of play. At century's end the best Negro players, then isolated into separate leagues, made closer to five hundred dollars, but it is likely that Walker, at least while with Toledo, rivaled his white teammates for pay. In midsummer the *Sporting Life* mused that "Columbus has a deaf mute and Cleveland a one-armed pitcher, Toledo a colored catcher and Providence a deaf centre-fielder; and yet these men can earn about $2,000 per annum apiece."[32] Such a lordly sum was likely to keep even an ailing catcher in reasonably good spirits, especially since early August brought Bella and Fleet a "little new catcher" to support, the eleven-pound Thomas Fleetwood Walker.[33]

Other favorable circumstances complemented the pay. Generally, the press praised Walker during his two seasons with Toledo, regarding him as refined, good-natured, and talented, though, of course, colored. Even in racially tense Cincinnati and St. Louis, the local papers echoed the *Sporting Life*'s opinion that "Toledo's colored catcher is looming up as a great man behind the bat."[34] The *St. Louis Globe-Democrat* went so far as to describe Walker's catching as "magnificent" and his throwing as "never excelled" in that city.[35] The *Toledo Blade* was generous to a fault with its coverage of Walker. While it made note of his errors, once judging his play as "miserable" and once as a "trifle off," it tempered criticism with understanding dismissals like, "The best have their off days," and reminders of "what he was in the time of our adversity, as well as for what he is." The *Blade*'s overall assessment of Walker's long 1883 season was glowing: "Walker has played more games and has been of greater value behind the bat than any catcher in the league."[36]

Additionally, though the Northwestern League's franchises were in midsized cities – Peoria, Quincy, and Springfield, Illinois; Bay City, Grand Rapids, and Saginaw, Michigan; and Fort Wayne, Indiana – exhibitions and connecting travel carried the Blue Stockings to and through major cities where players could enhance their reputations for wasting money on the pursuit of laughter and good times. The *Columbus Journal* noted that just before he broke his thumb, Walker's popularity among his teammates owed at least in part to yet one more of his talents. While marking time between games, he had regaled his team with "excellent" piano solos at a Columbus club room.[37]

His celebrity also led to new acquaintances. Fleet and Bella spent time as the guests of Archie Allen, a Toledo hotel and saloon keeper, and, when in Cincinnati, a trio of local notables squired Fleet around the city. His schedule likely allowed him to renew acquaintances with old friends as well. When he breezed through Oberlin, he did more than offer tips to young ballplayers. He also visited Ednah Mason. And twice in the latter months of 1883 the Toledo correspondent of the *Cleveland Gazette* noted that Ednah was visiting the city, once for several weeks during what should have been her fall semester at Oberlin.[38]

The drawback to the large salaries, the big-city travel, and the attractive social life was that a large number of open dates during the summer dictated that teams schedule a substantial number of exhibition games, even against teams from competing leagues. During Fleet Walker's career, these exhibitions would set up four encounters symbolic of the increasingly tense nature of race relations in baseball. All involved Adrian "Cap" Anson. The first came during the 1883 season, puncturing any illusions that high pay, good times, and excitement might have been encouraging in Walker.

Anson was the nineteenth century's greatest hitter and a colorful player later blamed for figuring prominently in baseball's ouster of blacks. In 1883, though his legend was just incubating, Anson was already widely recognized as the large, loud, and intimidating manager of the talented

Chicago White Stockings. When he brought his National League team to Toledo in August for an exhibition game, he announced that they would not play if Walker was in the lineup. This stance surprised the *Toledo Blade,* which observed tongue in cheek that when the White Stockings had arrived at the Union depot, they were mistaken initially for Haverly's Mastadons [*sic*] or Callendar's Consolidated, two black teams. Apparently, the Chicagoans' sunburned faces left it "a matter of doubt as to their being tainted with black blood."[39]

Charlie Morton, who had replaced Voltz as the Toledo manager at midseason, had not planned on playing Walker, who was nursing sore hands. Challenged by Anson's ultimatum, however, Morton put Walker in right field, daring Anson to risk forfeiture of the gate receipts. Anson is alleged to have said, "We'll play this here game, but won't play never no more with the nigger in."[40] The White Stockings, whose second baseman was Fritz Pfeffer, one of the Louisville players who had stalked off the field during Walker's warmup in Louisville in 1881, won 7–6 in front of a large crowd. Walker played an errorless game and scored a run, but his reactions went unrecorded. The incident turned out to be a portent of larger challenges yet ahead, but at that moment it appeared as just a bump in what was otherwise a season of auspicious beginnings.

When Morton had replaced Voltz, who eventually returned to sportswriting, Toledo was in fifth place. By early July, the Blue Stockings had risen to second, and a month later they were atop the Northwestern League. They finished the season as champions, two games ahead of Saginaw. If the management held to their end of a July offer, the finish among the league's top three teams earned each player a suit and an overcoat,[41] a bonus that their fashion-conscious catcher likely scrutinized closely. Reneging on the offer would have been an improbability. The team's success had made the front office financially flush and competitively overconfident. In exhibition they had beaten all of their American Association opponents and several National League teams. The *Sporting Life* implied that they were too much for the Northwestern League. At the heart of their ability, their correspondent wrote, were pitcher Hank O'Day and catcher Walker. Walker hit just .251 in 60 games, but with O'Day (who later became a well-known professional umpire) he formed "one of the most remarkable batteries in the country."[42] It was thus no surprise when Toledo's fine play encouraged the team to move in 1884 to the American Association, and no surprise that Fleet Walker was one of the minority of players that the club retained. The spotlight was about to shine a little brighter on the mulatto catcher.

Other blacks had played, were playing, and would continue to play professional ball, but in 1884 Walker became the first of them in a major league. The American Association had been formed in the winter of 1881 with the avowed intent to become a major league rival to the National League, a status it won with an 1882 agreement meant to keep them from raiding National League rosters.[43] While it was sometimes derided as the Beer-Ball League because some of its team owners were brewmasters and others sat on brewery boards of directors, the Association deliberately sought to distance itself from the problems that the public associated with baseball's destructive professional spirit – the gambling, drinking, and cheating. Though the league sold beer on park grounds, scheduled Sunday games, and halved the fifty-cent admission charge of the National League, it also set tough punishments for drinking players and attempted to create an atmosphere suitable for female spectators. A heightened emphasis on decorum could only make life easier for a collegian like Walker.

Further, baseball's emerging place in the pantheon of public entertainment would challenge and reward the showman in Walker. He was playing in an age that demanded a balance between panache and order, an age in which geeks, freaks, and other thrill-seeks competed with traditional fare for expanding leisure time and money. The traveling circus, experimentations with nighttime amusements made possible by electric lights, theater troupes, Wild West shows, and exhibitionists like marathon cyclist Elsie von Blumen, who had appeared in New Castle during Walker's stay, were signs of a culture that was beginning to blur the lines between celebrity and achievement.

Baseball fostered the blurring. Packaged as instant tradition – the national pastime that had grown from rural roots – it sought to distance itself from the seedier aspects of spectacle; things like crowds that chased umpires with guns, players who carried pitchers of beer onto the field with them, and rickety wooden bleachers whose collapse left many injured. At the same time, player uniforms grew increasingly colorful (Walker's Blue Stockings wore blue shirts and white pants), and experimentation with night baseball, begun early in the 1880s, indicated that the sport was not averse to tapping into the dollars that evening pleasure-seekers were spending on entertainment. One of the game's best players, Mike "King" Kelly, of Anson's Chicago White Stockings, symbolized the merging of sport and entertainment. He took an occasional stab at vaudeville, and his playing behavior reflected the short distance between the stage and the diamond. Lionized in popular song, Kelly was known to have run directly from first to third base when the umpire was not looking and once to have secured a victory by convincingly appearing to have caught a fly ball that actually flew many feet over his head. Fleet Walker's turn at the piano may not have put him in Kelly's league, but it did foreshadow his involvement in the performing arts. At the time, Negroes were not yet accorded the place that patronizing whites would later reserve for them as entertainers. How far could a handsome, light-skinned mulatto rise in the new pantheon of public notables? Walker would begin to find out in 1884.

Toledo's schedule that year called for another exhibition with Anson's White Stockings and for more than eight thousand miles of travel that would return Walker to Louisville and carry him repeatedly into the hostile environs of other Southern cities. When the season began, those possible conflicts were just clouds on the horizon. Playing at home in an exhibition against Cleveland, Walker had the first basehit for the now-major league Toledo team and scored the first run. The *Blade* continued the praise of the previous season, calling Walker "a daisy" and noting that he "handles the foul tips with an ease rarely excelled."[44]

It did not take long, however, for the dark clouds to drift in from the horizon and settle over Walker. Just two weeks after his successful debut he found himself in Louisville as the object of considerable attention. While the *Blade* remained loyally sympathetic throughout the season, and while the national *Sporting Life* decried overt racial incidents, other papers, particularly in the South, engaged in a constant – sometimes savage – campaign to denigrate Walker.

The sniping began with the season's 1 May opener in Louisville. During the week before Toledo's arrival the local *Commercial,* which, like nearly all Southern papers of the time, had no compunctions about running want ads that sought "colored boys" for menial physical jobs, stated that since other cities had accepted Walker, Louisville ought to have no objections to his play. Of course, they also mentioned that a refusal to play against Walker would mean forfeiture and a five-hundred-dollar fine for the Louisville club.

The day before the game, despite ridiculing the National Colored Convention delegates then meeting in Louisville as noisy, contentious speakers who wasted their time arguing over "'pints' of order," the *Commercial* wrote that Walker "enjoys the honor of being the first real brunette in the profession. He can play good ball behind the bat, and is a skillful thrower to bases."[45] It was a setup. When Walker committed five errors and went hitless the next day, one of the headlines read, "The Negro Catcher's Disastrous Errors." The game account then linked him to the Negro political convention, to the basest stereotypes of Negro character, and to the white hopes for black athletic incompetence:

(Toledo) had their Republican brunette, Walker, behind the bat and the poor fellow's mind was so much taken up with the State Republican Convention that he forgot he was playing baseball, fancied he was a Ninthward delegate with a razor in his pocket and fired the balls down to second base at such a disastrous angle that the Democrats of the home team easily stuffed the ballot box and ran off with the nomination. The colored brother found the polls closed in his face in the fourth inning and will be compelled to wait until the next election to get his vote in.[46]

The rest of the league's press was less overt in their hostilities, occasionally praising him, though the *St. Louis Globe-Democrat* also attributed several Toledo losses to the play of their "colored catcher," and the *Baltimore Sun* deemed his play "hardly satisfactory," despite some "wild pitching to handle" and "some marvelous stops."[47]

Fans came in many stripes. Spectators in all cities, even Louisville, St. Louis, and Cincinnati, applauded Walker on occasion. Colored spectators attended road games to cheer him, endowing Toledo with unexpected fans in their opponents' parks. Toledo, in fact, consistently drew good crowds for their series openers in other cities. Since the team was not contending for the pennant it is likely that much of the interest stemmed from Walker's presence. It was decidedly so in the South. In September, four Richmond fans tried to prevent his appearance there by sending a letter to manager Morton that read:

> We the undersigned do hereby warn you not to put up Walker, the negro catcher, the evenings that you play in Richmond, as we could mention the names of 75 determined men who have sworn to mob Walker if he comes on the ground in a suit. We hope you will listen to our words of warning, so there will be no trouble; but if you do not there certainly will be. We only write this to prevent much bloodshed, as you alone can prevent.

According to *Sporting Life*'s Richmond correspondent, the senders did not have names belonging to any Richmond residents.[48] Further, Walker was injured and probably would not have appeared there anyway. Perhaps he was never even aware of the letter.

The second episode with Cap Anson may have similarly been unknown to Walker. In April, Morton had agreed to another exhibition with Chicago and had offered assurances beforehand that Walker would not play. Chicago's secretary wrote to Morton, hoping to insure compliance by reminding the Toledo manager of the agreed-upon terms: "no colored man shall play in your nine and if your officers insist on playing him after we are there you forfeit the Guarantee and we refuse to play. Now I think this is fair as we refuse point blank to play colored men."[49] The game was eventually canceled, and both Anson and Walker were spared a confrontation. In an age when duels were still reported in the South and Northern gentlemen still administered beatings to one another over perceived slights, it was no small blessing to avoid trouble. In this case, it was merely deferred. More clashes with Anson awaited, though not that year.

While public controversy was not always the outcome, the 1884 season had to imbue Walker with the realization that day in and day out he was taking the field with and against players who did not want him to be there. Cap Anson was not an aberration. Curt Welch, a Toledo teammate who had grown up in East Liverpool, Ohio, a short distance from Steubenville, was an ardent segregationist.[50] More importantly, throughout 1884 Walker caught Toledo's outstanding pitcher, Tony Mullane. Several times, the *Toledo Blade* commented on Walker's inability to hold the charismatic, powerful pitcher. Though the paper deemed Walker an "excellent catcher," it also pronounced him "too light" for the job, asserting that Toledo's chances for a win would improve by fifty percent with a batterymate who could handle Mullane.[51] Apparently Walker was the only one privy that year to a secret that Mullane revealed decades later:

> He [Walker] was the best catcher I ever worked with, but I disliked a Negro and whenever I had to pitch to him I used to pitch anything I wanted without looking at his signals. One day he signalled me for a curve and I shot a fast ball at him. He caught it and walked down to me. He said, "I'll catch you without signals, but I won't catch you if you are going to cross me when I give you signals." And all the rest of that season he caught me and caught anything I pitched without knowing what was coming.[52]

The final irony of this association between the mulatto catcher and the intolerant Irishman is that in nearly all of the forty-two games that Walker played in 1884, Mullane was the pitcher. Despite its secret flaw, the battery was effective enough to spur the *Cleveland Gazette* to truism: "Just give Walker and Mullane the bat, and the Toledo nine will get 'thar' every time."[53]

It is an easy matter to explain Mullane and Anson and Welch and their mutual dislike of blacks by presenting them as poor whites for whom, in an ideologically classless society, white skin was their only perceived guarantee that they were better off than somebody else.[54] No doubt this is part of the explanation. A dashing figure rumored to be the inspiration for Ladies' Days at the ballpark (whether this is so, Toledo did set aside several games in 1884 for which women accompanied by men were admitted free), Tony Mullane had more victories (285) than any other pitcher not in the Hall of Fame. But he was born in Cork, Ireland, unschooled in any radical American notions of equality, and his un-ending tendency toward meanness, as evidenced by many brushback pitches, earned him *Sporting Life*'s characterization as "a man of the most sordid nature."[55]

Anson came from a family that had settled in Iowa among Pot-tawotami Indians and he was twice sent to boarding schools for disci-plinary reasons. Drinking and barroom brawls were regular features of his early days as a professional player. An apocryphal story from those days finds the young Adrian Anson so intent on playing in a big game that he dyes his hair and stains his skin to avoid recognition as a ringer. Though it is said that his father thwarted the scheme, the image of Anson darkening his face to play ball is an ironic one next to that of Anson a decade later, a man determined to prevent those with dark faces from playing.[56] It seems certain that Anson would not recognize the irony. He and Mullane were representative of those at whom "scientific" racism was pointed, whites who could be encouraged by a tissue of lies to define blacks as a different and lower species. Or perhaps, giving them the benefit of the doubt, they mirrored the more patronizing view that sought to remove blacks from bitter competition for the good of the Negro race. After all, Senator John T. Morgan, of Alabama was arguing just that year that black advances would be potentially disastrous. "The greater their personal success may be," he wrote, "the more they will feel the pressure of caste." The only hope for Negro achievement, according to Morgan, was through flight to Africa.[57] His suggestion closely coin-cided in time with that of Baltimore's Bishop Henry M. Turner, a black man who made the front page of the *New York Times* with his prediction of a great future nation in Africa comprised of American emigrants.[58] It is doubtful Anson and Mullane knew of John Morgan's proposition or Henry Turner's prophecy – it is impossible that Moses Fleetwood Walker was not familiar with both.

Despite the potential for friction that lay with writers, fans, contrac-tual agreements, opponents, and teammates, the chore of catching ex-acted the greatest toll from Walker in 1884. Several injuries disabled him for many games. He had just 152 at bats in a 104 game season. His .263 average put him among the top third of the league's hitters, but his thirty-seven errors placed him near the bottom of the league's thirty-three catchers.[59] The entire team, on its way to an eighth-place finish, was injury wracked, a circumstance that resulted in the recruitment of Weldy Walker for six appearances in the outfield. Heavily in debt by season's end, Toledo sought to relieve itself of expensive contracts. Fleet had never fully recovered from a rib broken in July (chest protectors were just that season coming into general use, though they would still be struggling for acceptance into the 1890s). In early August he returned to the lineup in centerfield, still too lame to go behind the plate. His injuries made his October release from the club an expected one. Toledo's *Sporting Life* correspondent bid Walker a gracious farewell in print, attributing his release to his unfortunate injuries. "By his fine, gentlemanly deportment," he wrote, Walker "has made a host of friends who will regret to learn that he is no longer a member of the club."[60]

Perhaps prematurely resigned to life without careers in baseball or law, Walker, graciously labeled a subgraduate of the University of Michigan by the Negro newspaper the *Cleveland Gazette,* took a job in December 1884 as a U.S. Postal Service clerk in Toledo.[61] When Fleet accepted a position beneath his talents, the moment provided a rare, albeit brief, instance in which brother Weldy's ambition burned a bit brighter. In October of that year Weldy and a partner assumed operation of the Delmonico Dining Rooms in Mingo, near Steubenville.[62] Of greater note was his entanglement in a legal issue of race separation.

Among the new phenomena competing for the dollars Americans were spending on entertainment in 1884 were roller rinks. Steubenville, with three new rinks, shared the national fever, and thus also became vulnerable to the issues of race and conduct that they raised. The intimacy of the rinks made them fearsome affronts to social propriety. In October 1884, New Jersey ministers railed against them in sermons. The newspaper ad for one of the Steubenville rinks carried a caveat: "the Rink will be conducted in a proper manner. No improper persons will be admitted. None but gentlemen and ladies need apply for admittance, to whom we extend a cordial invitation."[63]

To define *improper,* or *gentlemen* and *ladies,* one began with skin color. The *Cleveland Gazette* claimed that the Steubenville rinks had issued the edict, "No Negroes need apply except for positions of menials," a pronouncement the paper said broke with Steubenville's understood tradition of nondiscrimination.[64] In actuality, though black couples were frequenting the town's Opera House without incident, Steubenville's whites still defined the limits of interracial social contacts. What differentiated an opera house from a roller rink? Well, black patrons of the first were likely to be of middle-class means, and, more important, already coupled. On the other hand, the roller rink invited young, single persons to revel in a social whirl rife with frivolity, relaxed moral standards, and physical contact. Race mixing in that setting was an explosive formula for regret. Best to keep the alien elements separated.

On the Friday before Halloween, when the third new rink opened on North Fifth Street, a full band playing as thousands of gas jets illuminated what the *Daily Herald* touted as the "most attractive place in the city," it had already been made clear that there would be no blacks among the eight hundred of Steubenville's "best people" in attendance.[65] This was because two weeks prior Weldy Walker and a friend, Hannibal Lyons, the son of a barber and family friend of the Walkers from Mount Pleasant, had already attempted unsuccessfully to integrate the other two rinks. Told by the proprietor of the South Side Rink, "You are colored and you can't skate," Walker and Lyons brought suit. The case stirred interest in the black community. It was resolved in the manner that would increasingly demonstrate the North's ambivalent approach to race relations. The court awarded Walker and Lyons fifteen dollars each in damages, a judgment that nominally supported integration while doing nothing to promote it in everyday reality. The rinks were not commanded to admit Negroes.[66]

Both the *Steubenville Gazette* and the *Ohio Press* implied that Walker and Lyons were troublemakers stirring a "political and social racket," absurdly mixing the social with the civil law, and trying "to control one by the other." The papers opted for this view, according to the *Cleveland Gazette,* because both papers were fearful of losing the support of black voters as spring elections neared, but equally afraid of losing the ads of the rink proprietors.[67]

At the same time that Weldy was bringing suit, his older brother William was contributing his own challenge to the once-settled nature of Steubenville relations. The town's correspondent to the *Pittsburgh Leader* wrote of a "scandal" on Christmas night of 1884 at Walker's saloon, prattling about "a white woman there who has gotten so low in the moral scale as to be content to associate with colored people." William would punctuate this scandalous bit of race mixing when, in 1894, at the age of forty-seven he married Maud Murray, a twenty-two-year-old white woman.[68]

Though Fleet Walker had no part in either incident involving his brothers, both spoke volumes about the developments in race relations that would invite future challenges to his own public deportment. In retrospect, the *Toledo Blade*'s unguarded praise of Walker's character at the end of the 1884 season carried a heavy dose of irony. In midseason the *Sporting Life* had cited the Toledo team for less "kicking and monkeying... than any club we have ever seen."[69] Yet, in a league taking great care with its public reputation, there had been problems with alcohol. Though the *Blade* retracted an accusation of player drunkenness that it had printed in July, in late September the Toledo management fined two players for the same offense.[70] Moses Fleetwood Walker's indulgence in liquor could have begun at any time – in the back alleys of his Steubenville youth, at Oberlin amid the timeless reverie of college students, in offseason moments spent at his brother's saloon, during his moments as the ballplaying guest of saloon keepers, or during the many hours that professional athletes need to kill between their fixes of competition. Walker may or may not have been among those that Toledo suspended – the club did not make public the names – but by the time his playing career, which resumed in 1885, ended some five years hence, he was definitely acquainted with drink, an affinity that would eventually challenge his public reputation.

In that half decade, the question of character would become increasingly vital to Walker's tightrope walk through professional baseball. Though the 1884 season with Toledo marked the last time in sixty-three years that a black man would be a major leaguer, Fleet was far from finished with his testing of racial ideology. White leagues would continue to act as his crucible even as social pressures – and he himself – turned up the flame.

3

. . . .

It is stated upon good authority that the negro catcher,

Walker, doesn't carry a razor and it will be unnecessary

to search him at the gate today.

Louisville Commercial, 3 May 1884

LEFT LIKE ALEXANDER, WITHOUT A WORLD TO CONQUER

In May 1888 Fleet Walker was still catching baseballs for a living, but he had decided by that time to become less benign about fielding insults and other perceived affronts. Now in his sixth season of high-level professional play, Walker was in Toronto, Canada, with his new team, the Syracuse Stars. After catching in the first two losses of the series he came to the park for the third game in street clothes and sat on the bench next to his manager. In the fourth inning the Stars' third baseman asked the umpire to remove some spectators who had taken a position in foul territory on the playing side of a restraining fence. Toronto's manager, Charlie Cushman, in crossing the field to move the fans, noticed Walker on the bench and for some reason ordered him to leave as well. Indignant, Walker left after engaging in heated words, first with Cushman and then with Toronto fans. The latter was not a good idea in light of the reputation of Toronto fans. Just a few days before, some toughs at the Toronto park had stolen the bases right off the diamond, and the club's directors were also attempting to put an end to the penchant some spectators had for throwing cushions onto the field during play. On this particular day, fan hostility heightened when Walker arrived behind the stands. There, a previously undocumented side of the Syracuse catcher made its public emergence. In short time two detectives, having found a loaded revolver on Walker, had arrested him.[1]

48

Toronto's *Globe,* which described Walker in a subheadline as a "war-like ballplayer," said the catcher had threatened to put a hole in Cushman. The *Toronto Daily Mail* reported that at one point, when it appeared that he might be assaulted, Walker had threatened to shoot but had made no attempt to draw his gun. The usually sympathetic *Sporting Life* presented two versions, those of their Toronto and Syracuse correspondents. The first wrote that Walker "flourished a loaded (six-chambered) revolver and talked of putting a hole in someone in the crowd." The latter dismissed the weapon as a "pop-gun" and maintained that "if the hoodlums in the Toronto audience had one-third the gentlemanly qualities that Walker possesses there would never be a disturbance at ball games." By all accounts, Walker wound up under arrest at the city's Station No. 4. Whether he made his bail of two hundred dollars or spent the night in jail, his gun was impounded and a fine was levied. One day later Walker was in the Stars' lineup in Hamilton, Ontario, though the *Daily Mail*'s baseball notes observed cryptically that the Syracuse manager was looking for another catcher.[2]

It was the first time that the rage in Fleet Walker had brought forth a weapon, but the events of his career since leaving Toledo in 1884 had already exposed him to the experience of being arrested, and the geographical range of his baseball travels had no doubt inspired both deepening concerns for his safety and a less humble bearing in dealing with them. They certainly never spurred in him a lessened resolve to play in predominantly white leagues. Taken in concert, all those things resulted in little denunciation from those reporting the Toronto incident, as if the newspapermen understood a loaded revolver to be a natural response to Walker's unique plight. None of them realized that, natural or not, it signaled that Fleet Walker's good-natured public demeanor was fraying, a process begun with his slide from the exhilarating heights of major league ball.

The broken rib which essentially ended Walker's 1884 season had threatened to make him the earliest forerunner of Wally Pipp, the New York Yankee who yielded his position at first base one day in 1925 and never got it back when his replacement, Lou Gehrig, went on to play in a record-setting 2,130 consecutive games. Toledo had replaced Walker at catcher with another Ohioan, James "Deacon" McGuire. McGuire hit only .185 as Walker's replacement, but he stayed behind the plate for another twenty-five major league seasons, a feat of durability to challenge Gehrig's. Walker, however, diverted from Pipp's path. When cast off by financially reeling Toledo (the team folded soon thereafter) at the close of the 1884 season, Walker spent the winter as a mail clerk, but signed to play with Cleveland of the Western League for the summer of 1885. Before the team's June withdrawal from the league, which itself disbanded a short time later, Walker hit .279 in eighteen games. The city's *Plain Dealer* thought highly of his catching. It noted that against his former team, Walker had handled "rather wild and very speedy balls finely" and had given Toledo "notice that the second bag was too well-watched to steal."[3]

The stay in Cleveland, brief as it was, also forced Walker into further tests of mettle in racially tense situations. Now four years from his initial, shaky debut with the White Sewing Machine Company team, and steeled by Toledo's travels to Baltimore, Louisville, Richmond, St. Louis, and Washington, D.C., Walker ventured deep into the Old South with his new team. The club began their season with a trip that swung them through Atlanta and Macon, Georgia, Chattanooga and Memphis, Tennessee, and into Birmingham, Alabama. The trip brought him within one day of the lynching of a Negro in Chattanooga and within one day of a visit by Cap Anson and the White Stockings to Atlanta.[4] Not only did Walker play during this road series, he played well, drawing compliments from Cleveland's *Sporting Life* correspondent for his hitting and catching.[5] But Cleveland gave him less in the way of baseball than it did in other matters of interest to him, rekindling enthusiasm for the law profession and providing him his first experience in running a public place dependent on dollars spent in leisure.

If he had once decided to abandon his law career, his Cleveland experience renewed its possibilities. In retrospect, the renewal may have had little positive to recommend it, another case of pouring time and faith into an institution that would dispense false hope rather than justice. Without question, however, an 1885 incident demonstrated that Walker was not reluctant to participate in the judicial process.

On Sunday, 19 April, Cleveland officials had warned its Western League team not to violate the city ordinance against playing games on the Sabbath. The team played nonetheless, and a warrant was issued the following day. Returning from an away game at Toledo, the subject of that warrant, Moses Fleetwood Walker, surrendered himself to police. The team had arranged to offer their budding lawyer-catcher in place of the manager. It was not an uncommon occurrence for a catcher to act as the symbolic fall guy in municipal wrangling over the Sunday baseball issue. Walker's possible penalty was a fine not to exceed twenty-five dollars and/or imprisonment in a workhouse for no longer than thirty days. As agreed, however, Walker was quickly freed on bail to await a trial that was to be a test case for Sunday ball, rather than an earnest effort to pass sentence on a player.[6]

The trial began on 30 April. The team hired two attorneys, Virgil P. Kline and J. L. Athey, to defend Walker. They asked for dismissal of his case, arguing that the section of the municipal code allegedly violated rested on the intent to keep order. The baseball game, they asserted, caused no disturbance. It was, in fact, as legitimate as the Sunday comic operas performed in the city. That, interjected the judge, was the case "supposing it to be a good game." Walker's attorney asserted that it was a good game and received surprising corroboration. "Yes, it was a good game," agreed the city prosecutor. "I saw it." Athey's summation went to the heart of the issue: class and morals. Baseball, he said, was a productive activity bolstered by the team's prohibitions against gambling and alcohol. He did not mention that streetcar monopolist, Tom Jonston, was at the bottom of the Sunday ball scheme, or that the games were expected to draw "like some strong plaster."[7] They might have drawn best among the working classes, those who could not attend games any other day. If the working classes became a regular core of fans, not only would Cleveland's pietistic Sabbatarians be genuinely offended, baseball as a privilege of the respectable classes would be negated as well.

Walker and the team won a victory on 3 May. The judge held that the code specifically banned only marbles and quoits. Whether baseball was another "game or sport" as outlined in the code was a matter for legislative, not judicial reckoning. The victory was short-lived. Two weeks later authorities arrested Cleveland's other catcher, J. A. Sommers. His eventual jury conviction under state rather than city statute helped to delay Sunday baseball in Cleveland until 1910. It made the city one of the few metropolitan areas to resist the widespread acceptance of play on the Lord's day.[8] For Fleet Walker, the brush with jurisprudence seemed to inspire a hunger for more, to encourage a reckless faith in legal matters that would continue in the years ahead.

When the Cleveland club, just one of several financially failing Western League teams, closed shop in June, Fleet Walker moved on to Waterbury, Connecticut, to play ball in a park "chopped out of a virgin forest" and set down in the middle of a swamp.[9] Walker played ten games for Waterbury in 1885 in the Southern New England League, time enough for the local press to praise him as "the people's choice." When the season ended, the paper reported that Walker was returning to Ann Arbor's law school, adding the wishful distortion, "He will graduate this year."[10] Michigan's records do not support the claims. His actual off-season whereabouts became evident when the Steubenville correspondent of the *Cleveland Gazette* revealed that Walker was the proprietor of the LeGrande House in Cleveland, a building that doubled as theater and opera house. Weldy, who had sold his Mingo restaurant after just six months, assisted him with the LeGrande.[11] The undertaking greatly affected Fleet's twilight years. He would later choose to retire in Cleveland; eventually, he would die there. In 1885, however, there was no time for sinking roots.

He returned to Waterbury for the entire 1886 season when the team joined the more competitive Eastern League. He played in only thirty-five games the second year, hitting just .218 and committing thirty-seven errors.[12] The time in Waterbury was uneventful, but it proved to be just a lull sandwiched between the excitement of Toledo and what lay ahead. Despite the desultory performances of 1885 and 1886, Fleet Walker nonetheless found employment in 1887 in another white league – and one of higher caliber – an extraordinary testament to his ability to survive inasmuch as the social pressure for segregation had by now necessitated a separate black baseball experience. The formal division was a dark foreboding, a signal that public belief was rapidly transforming racial lore into the deeper conviction of an ideology.

Records of baseball games between all-black clubs stretch back to at least 1862. By the early 1880s a movement had begun that created dozens of all-Negro teams. Weldy Walker played with one such team in Pittsburgh. Though a few attempts at forming all-Negro leagues failed between 1885 and 1895, the urge or the need to separate the races was evident. When the first segregated team to rise to prominence began play in 1886, they had already decided it was advantageous to avoid the stigma of identification as American Negroes, and thus named themselves the Cuban Giants. One recounting says that they spoke gibberish on the field in the hope that it sounded Spanish. The players, most of the finest Negro players in the country, received twelve to eighteen dollars weekly.[13]

In 1887 Fleet Walker could no longer command the two-thousand-dollar salary of a major leaguer. Still, he could earn in the neighborhood of two hundred dollars monthly in the high minor leagues. It is no wonder, then, that Fleet Walker chose the substantially larger income and acclaim of the white leagues. While *The Sporting News* gleefully noted that Walker's former nemesis, Tony Mullane, was pitching for a "jay club" in far off Vermont in 1887 (and wishfully commanded him to "stay there"),[14] Walker had the luxury of remaining that year in the upper echelons of white ball. The 1887 season became Fleet Walker's baseball roller coaster ride, its ups and downs both recalling his previous heights and foreshadowing his future troubles. That he took the ride at all owed largely to two other men, Charley Hackett and George Washington Stovey.

Newark, of the powerful International League, had hired Hackett, Walker's Waterbury manager, for the 1887 season. Whatever the Waterbury statistics may have said about Walker's abilities, Hackett thought enough remained to take Fleet with him. In an assessment that would later prove paradoxical, Hackett thought that Walker's character, and probably color, would have a good influence on a pitcher new to the Newark team, George Stovey. Stovey's Jersey City manager of the previous year, though he had spirited Stovey away from Trenton with twenty dollars and a new suit for a single game against Newark,[15] regarded the black lefthander as "headstrong and obstinate, and, consequently, hard to manage." The *Newark Daily Journal* disputed this, terming Stovey "very gentlemanly" and a "first class lad to work with." Even so, the paper admitted to the hope that "Walker will develop him further."[16] Social graces and temperament aside, there was no question about Stovey's talents. He had played briefly with the Cuban Giants, and one writer called him "the brunette fellow with the sinister fin and the demonic delivery." His breaking ball was so good that the writer asked, "What's the use of bucking against a fellow that can throw at the flagstaff and make it curve into the water pail?" His deliveries looked "as large as an alderman's opinion of himself," but when they arrived could not be hit "with a cellar door."[17]

Stovey and Walker proved to be a popular and effective pair. Publicly billed as the Cuban, Spanish, mulatto, African, or Arabian battery, they attracted the large crowds that *Sporting Life*'s Newark correspondent had predicted before the season began. "Verily they are dark horses," he had written, "and ought to be a drawing card. No rainchecks given when they play."[18]

From most perspectives, it was a good match. Stovey tested Walker's restraint at times. Once, when the catcher believed several passed balls owed to Stovey's irascibility, he "tired of the business, . . . and showed it plainly by his manner."[19] Their cooperation and talent overcame such minor incidents. Stovey won thirty-five games, an International League record, and Walker hit .264 while impressing writers with "exceedingly clever" and steady work in the field. One claimed that there "might have been a river ten feet behind him and not a ball would have gone into it." Another honored Walker with a poem:

> There is a catcher named Walker
> Who behind the bat is a corker,
> He throws to a base
> With ease and with grace,
> And steals 'round the bags like a stalker.[20]

Deemed a "colored Bushong" (after "Doc" Bushong, a dentist and catcher with a long career in professional ball), Walker was popular with Newark fans, impressing them with both nerve and manner. In an April game, after stealing both second and third bases, he made an unsuccessful dash for the plate, encouraged by the fact that the previous season he had scored using the same trick when the opposing pitcher had been "so astonished at Walker's audacity he did not think to put him out."[21] Of even greater audacity was an act in the season's final month, a courtesy born of good breeding that exposed the gap between Walker and most other players and between professional baseball of that era and future decades. While Walker was catching, a close decision at the plate went his way. When the opposing players stormed the umpire, Walker voluntarily admitted that he had not touched the runner.[22]

Perhaps the best indicator of how confident Walker was in 1887 appeared in a small press item at the end of April: "Walker of the Newarks," it said, "umpired the game."[23] A catcher standing in as umpire was not earthshaking in 1880s baseball. Still, it would have been a bold move for any mulatto less self-assured and less drawn to the spotlight than Fleet Walker.

While praise often followed him, however, there remained contrary events that must have left him privately seething and humiliated. For one, some newspapers were still ladling out racial invective. As a sprained ankle left him hobbling around on a cane, the *Hamilton (Ontario) Spectator* wrote that "Walker, the coon catcher of the Newarks, is laid off with a sore knee. It is insinuated by envious compeers that in early life he practiced on hen roosts until he got the art of foul catching down fine." While such blatant language drew challenges from other writers, one insisting that the author had to be Walker's inferior "in education, refinement, and manliness," it nonetheless reflected an audience of approving readers.[24]

Cap Anson and his White Stockings also continued their agitation for race separation. When the team rolled into Newark for an exhibition game on 14 July, it seemed a curious place for Anson to assert his dislike for Negroes. Certainly he knew that Walker and Stovey would be there. The International League, in fact, had become so hospitable to black players that the *Sporting Life* wondered if it would not soon become known as the "Colored League."[25] Buffalo's Frank Grant, a Negro, would be the league's leading hitter that year, and there were other talented blacks in the league. Still, Anson chose to press forward with his demands for segregation. As it would turn out, his attitudes were shared in 1887 by more whites than was sometimes apparent, and certainly the prestige of the White Stockings helped convert those feelings into authority. In this encounter, Anson proved the greater force. Newark did not play either Walker or Stovey. The latter had been scheduled to pitch, but complained the evening before of sickness.[26] The absence of the black battery drew no mention from the press. It was not until the next year that the *Sporting Life* reported that Stovey had not been the victim of illness, but rather of Anson's absolute refusal to share the field with colored players.[27]

According to former black star Sol White, Anson was also pivotal in keeping Walker from returning to the major leagues. Newark's "Spanish battery" so impressed John Montgomery Ward, the captain of the New York Giants, during a 3–2 exhibition loss — Walker having thrown out Ward in an attempted steal — that the Giants made an offer for both players. Hackett turned it down. Though it was a good sign that Walker's talents had not expired in Waterbury, Connecticut, Hackett's refusal may have been inconsequential. According to White's later claims, the potential sale had set off a howl "heard from Chicago to New York" that drew its strength from Anson's "strenuous and fruitful opposition."[28]

That Anson's bigotry had now gained a wider acceptance was a sad sign of how quickly the mix of racial ideology was setting. Many baseball observers have attempted to frame Anson as the single-handed villain in baseball's eventual decision to segregate. While this is wrong and trivializes the resistance to integrated play among a wide circle of players, in the case of Walker, Anson's impact was substantial. He apparently had kept the catcher from the major leagues in more than one instance. After Walker's death some three and one-half decades later, his obituary in Cleveland's black newspaper related that the owner of Cleveland's National League team had confided to the writer that he would have signed Walker but for the objections of Anson.[29]

Assuredly, the tenacity of Anson's racism was unsettling. The poisonous secrecy of its workings, though an obviously efficient way for whites to wrestle with the "colored problem," was doubly destructive. It seems fitting, then, that the day after Anson's petty triumph, the directors of the International League met secretly and, after discussion, directed their secretary to approve of no more contracts for colored players. Six teams, all without blacks, voted for the measure. Four teams, all with at least one black player, voted against. The press quickly found out. The *Newark Daily Journal* pronounced Moses F. Walker to be "mentally and morally the equal of any director who voted for the resolution."[30] As had been the case in Toledo, however, it was not the directors who objected most strenuously to blacks. Instead, it was at the behest of many of the best players, those who had to share the field with Fleet Walker and many of whom reportedly threatened to leave the league, that the International League decided to draw the color line.[31]

The betrayal of the formerly hospitable International League, the obstinacy of those like Anson, and the continuing public acceptance of racial labels affixed to players like Walker, Grant, and Stovey, meant that players of color could not continue to find suitable competition without forcing themselves into places where they were not wanted. The talented black athlete who refused to accept separate arrangements had become an affront to racial ideology, threatening on several levels. Obviously, the fact of direct competition was one. The possible economic displacement of whites, as in many trades, was another. But the speed with which blacks were hustled from the arenas of physical prowess in the 1880s and thereafter – from horse racing and cycling and pedestrianism and boxing and baseball – hinted at something stronger.

It seems likely that the meaning of black versus white athletic competition was again tied to white paranoia about black physical prowess and, ultimately, sexuality. The skilled and often triumphant black athlete graphically symbolized the unleashed power of black men, power that many whites feared could be turned insatiably toward the vulnerable community of white women. In no small way the implied sexual threat explained the turn-of-the-century hostility of whites toward heavyweight boxer Jack Johnson and his dalliances with white women. Even in less flammable circumstances, however, blacks were consistently denied access to municipal golf courses and swimming pools because city parks boards thought these facilities brought black men too close to white women.[32]

To lessen the threat, whites began constructing a myth of black athletic incapability, a physical version of the accepted public belief in inferior black intelligence. To match the tongue in cheek but all too serious denigrations of black intelligence that appeared in newspaper "humor" (example: the *Newark Daily Journal* reported that when rain began in the middle of a Cuban Giant game, one of the Giants dove for cover with the shout, "Scatter, men, de debil am spitting"),[33] occasional newspaper or magazine caricatures presented Negroes as athletically inept. The portrayals were wishful thinking, salve that could not heal the deep uneasiness with which whites regarded the reality of black athleticism. The reality leaked from little incidents such as those at Evansville, Indiana, in 1890. Foul balls there occasioned lively betting as to whether a white or black boy would win the race to retrieve the ball. "Big odds," a paper reported, "are given in favor of the black boy."[34] And it leapt from the larger presence of men like Fleet Walker on professional ball fields. The myth, then, would have to be built on the unbelievable but simple refusal of whites to compete against blacks.

While such a bald ploy, when asserted as evidence of white supremacy, could bring only hollow victory, it was preferable to running the risk of real defeat on the playing field. Boxing champion John L. Sullivan refused to fight Negroes, and now baseball would adopt his strategy. Blacks knew from the moment that they organized separate teams that there would be a price for defeating whites. When segregated teams were matched, even in little Ohio towns, and the "colored boys took the cake," the black teams were careful to keep the score down.[35] When blacks did well they heard whining and innuendo. In the pivotal 1887 season, Newark's *Daily Journal,* the same paper that backed Fleet Walker, reported that Buffalo's second baseman, Frank Grant, "will not do the 'circus act' unless there is a large crowd of spectators present."[36] Grant was thus doubly accused of the flamboyant showmanship that in the century ahead would stereotype black entertainers and of a trait that still stigmatizes black athletes in the late twentieth century – the inclination to compete with varying levels of intensity. The latter is one more manifestation of the myth of black incapability that has undergone subtle transformations in an effort to stay one step ahead of black athletic advances. They all rest on the foundation built of the decision of whites in the late 1880s to forgo interracial contact on the playing fields. So though he did not know it at the time, when Fleet Walker had left the University of Michigan to become a professional baseball player, he was positioned on the swell of a small wave. He rode it a very brief time before it broke and the undertow began to carry him, and other blacks, back toward where they had been.

Ironically, the wave had crested in 1887, when at least seven Negro players had good performances that season in competitive professional white leagues. While their good play was no obstacle to the *Toronto World*'s declaration that the presence of blacks had "not been productive of satisfactory results," their success spurred black ballplayer Bud Fowler's plans to unite them for an offseason tour of the South and West. The team, which never materialized, would have included, according to the *Sporting Life,* Stovey, Walker, Grant, Fowler, and five members of the Cuban Giants.[37] It might also have racially split professional baseball prematurely, though not by much.

As it turned out, it would take just two more tumultuous seasons to accomplish the de facto separation of white and black baseball players. A sympathetic backlash from the press and fans caused the International

League, which dissolved itself and reorganized as the International Association, to relax its color line in the offseason after 1887. As the 1888 season approached, the league settled informally on a general understanding that black players would be restricted – no more than one per team – but not altogether banned. Though Walker had struggled to the finish line of the 1887 season with the injuries (including a fractured collar bone) of an aging catcher, his return was expected to fill Newark's quota in 1888.

As had the fans and writers at most of his previous stops, Newark's baseball followers regarded Fleet Walker as refined and restrained. He was very much a gentleman, the *Daily Journal* reported, and "unwilling to force himself where he is not wanted."[38] It was a statement that revealed how little anyone knew of the riddle that was Fleet Walker. Although local newsmen had reported in August that Walker practiced law in Toledo during the winter and that he owned property worth twenty-five thousand dollars, they seemed to find nothing unusual in routinely mentioning in January that the catcher was in Newark packing sewing machines for export and staying sharp by tossing a claw hammer in the air and catching it while awaiting further word on the color line situation.[39] At the end of the season, there had been other confusion surrounding the degree of Walker's wealth. The rumored twenty-five thousand dollars in property had mysteriously shifted to Cleveland. The *Sporting Life* disavowed its existence, but a month later the Newark paper reported that Walker had purchased a cottage and six lots in the city's Irvington Park section.[40]

Newark's baseball aficionados were most confused, however, over the matter of Walker's intentions and his unwillingness to go where he was not wanted, for when the 1888 season opened he had signed with a new team in a place where many of his teammates made no secret of the fact that they did not want him. Newark's new manager added to the cries of duplicity that the spurned Newark fans heaped on Walker. He claimed that the day after he had agreed to run the club he had asked Walker if he would sign with Newark. He said that Walker promised he would open negotiations nowhere else if the color line issue was resolved. When Walker made the promise, the new manager accused, he had already committed himself to follow former manager Charley Hackett to the Syracuse Stars, an International Association rival.[41]

Syracuse became the only team permitted to keep two blacks on the roster for 1888 when they first signed Walker and sent him an advance four months prior to the season[42] and then re-signed pitcher Robert Higgins. The contracts were an enigma inasmuch as racial feeling had split the Syracuse Stars during the previous season. Before that 1887 season had even begun, in fact, controversy had arisen over whether a newly acquired catcher, Dick Male, was indeed a black named Dick Johnson. Male refuted the rumor, calling its instigator "himself a black liar." But following his release, after he had supposedly been run off the club, he turned up with Zanesville of the Ohio State League as Dick Johnson, a black catcher.[43]

Additionally, a group of players recruited from the defunct Southern League, the team's "Ku Klux coterie," had refused to support Higgins's pitching. In an exhibition with Toronto, they had intentionally muffed routine chances in the field, resulting in twenty-eight runs against Higgins. In midseason, two of them had refused to sit with Higgins for the team photograph. The more volatile of the two, Douglas "Dug" Crothers, explained later that "I would have my heart cut out before I would consent to have my picture in the group."[44]

During Fleet Walker's first season with Syracuse, hostility toward International Association blacks did not ease. Though Walker had threatened them two months earlier with a loaded revolver, Toronto crowds remained as virulent in 1888 as they had been a season before when they had done little more than blow their horns and shout at Buffalo's Frank Grant, "Kill the nigger."[45] Grant continued to be the frequent target of beanballs and vicious feet-first slides that had necessitated his move to the outfield. League umpires continued to be suspected of deciding close calls against teams with black players. A Baltimore writer told a Toronto counterpart in May that they had been beaten in Syracuse by "a coon battery." It was, he affirmed, a "hard dose to swallow."[46] Before the season ended, Higgins, despite having twenty wins, left the Stars, leaving Fleet Walker as the team's only Negro.

Cap Anson also haunted Fleet Walker one last time in 1888. Appearing in Syracuse for a September exhibition, he naturally refused, as always, to play against blacks. Unlike 1883, when Toledo had backed him down, Anson's policy was now so widely accepted that the white press did not even report his slight against Walker. Only the Negro press described Anson's demands for Walker's replacement, demands to which the Syracuse assent meant that "the big baby was satisfied."[47]

Oddly, relations among the Syracuse players may have actually improved a bit in 1888. The team won often, and the players were paid exorbitantly by league standards. With money scarce in general, baseball attendance was in nationwide decline. Though the first-place Stars were down at the gate from the previous year, the team's salary list amounted to nearly twenty thousand dollars when it should have been closer to thirteen thousand dollars.[48] And, though Higgins later left the club to return to his Memphis barbershop, both he and Walker were not without support. When the International Association had partially rescinded its color line, black citizens had written to thank the man who had represented the Stars at league meetings. Shortly before the season had begun, a group of blacks had feted Walker and Higgins with a banquet at the YMCA.[49] As would become clear later, Walker had also made a good impression on J. C. Bowe, one of the Syracuse club directors.

Among the players, Walker enjoyed the friendship of pitcher Con Murphy, a not altogether positive note, though perhaps a telling one. Murphy was a loose cannon, an example of the "hoodlum" ballplayer who was supposed to be extinct among professionals in the late 1880s. His name was as likely to pop up in an account of how a local wrestler had swept some barroom floor with his body as it was in connection with baseball. In 1887 he had earned a ten-dollar fine in a game for kicking about calls. He responded in his next at bat by waiting for the ball to be pitched and then leaping across the plate so that neither catcher nor umpire could see the ball. On his third leap he was fined twenty-five dollars and the ballgame was called in favor of the opposing team.[50] The best evidence of Walker's popularity came at the October banquet celebrating the team's International Association championship. Walker, though having hit just .170, served as unofficial spokesman for the team, thanking the Syracuse directors and citizens for their support.[51]

Walker felt comfortable enough in Syracuse to move there and open a business after the first season. The nature of the business, which he shared in partnership with a local umpire, is uncertain, but a clue was in the *Sporting Life*'s observation that it had held a "rousing opening" on Christmas Eve.[52] Perhaps another clue was in a seemingly lighthearted article printed in the same paper little more than a month later. Walker, it related, while returning from a business trip to Oswego, had met an acquaintance on the train. They had become engrossed in conversation, the time passing so "merrily" that, even though the train stopped for fifteen minutes scarcely two blocks from Walker's Syracuse home, he failed to get off, causing him an extra fifty miles of travel and an overnight stay in Cortland. The "considerable fun" that friends were having with Walker over the matter induced both passengers to "declare that they had nothing all day at Oswego but ginger ale and soda water."[53] Whatever the social whirl of the offseason may have promised, by the time the 1889 season opened, Syracuse's popular catcher was a far lonelier man.

Moses Fleetwood Walker was left to play the 1889 season as the last black in the International League until Jackie Robinson. Contract disputes led to the exodus of Grant and another black from the league. Higgins never returned to Syracuse. Walker did so for fifty games before his release on 23 August. A small newspaper item in the *Cleveland Gazette* near the end of the season punctuated the nadir. Former Oberlin and Toledo teammate Harlan Burket claimed many years later that hotels that refused Walker accommodations in 1883 and 1884 had forced the catcher to sleep on park benches and in railroad stations, acts to which he allegedly responded by filing lawsuits.[54] Municipal archives can not verify those filings, but in the last month of his final season of 1889 the *Gazette* confirmed that Walker and a friend had indeed entered suit against a Detroit restaurant that refused them service. The saddest hint to Walker's standing, however, was not in the lawsuit but in the closing line in which the editor, a friend of Walker's, felt compelled to add, "Wish Fleet would pay us a bill we have against him."[55] The tag begged for answers to implied questions: Had Walker acquired the unflattering knack of celebrity entitlement, or just the spendthrift ways of a man who thought his talents could outrun and outlast the cumulative debts of fast living?

Though Bud Fowler, George Stovey, and Frank Grant would play for many years with integrated teams, with all-Negro teams in white leagues, and with independent Negro teams,[56] Walker was finished with baseball. He had been the last black to play in a highly competitive, integrated league. What is more, it almost seemed as if he and the others had left of their own accord or ineptitude. Both Walker and the Stars had slumped in 1889. At the time of his release, Walker was hitting .216 and was twentieth among the league's twenty-one catchers defensively.

The disappearance of blacks from white leagues drew more eulogies than outrage. An anonymous International League player offered *The Sporting News* a patronizing explanation that made it seem as if the color line would be a good thing for beleaguered black players: "While I myself am prejudiced against playing in a team with a colored player," he said, "still I could not help pitying some of the poor black fellows that played in the International League." He went on to lament the fact that Fowler had needed wooden shin guards to protect himself while playing second base.[57] And while many newspapermen wrote pietistically about particular "gentlemanly" black players, few seemed to grasp the overarching implications of blanket segregation. The *Sporting Life* in 1887 had concluded that players in an experimental colored league would not require contractual protection from the white leagues because "there is not likely to be much of a scramble for colored players. Only two such players are now employed in professional white clubs, and the number is not likely to be ever materially increased owing to the high standard of play required and to the popular prejudice against any considerable mixture of races."[58] So there it was – the absence of blacks owed not exclusively to a relentless social squeeze nor to legal attempts to banish them, but to the cause most comforting to whites: blacks were not talented enough for such a high standard of play.

The popularity of baseball promoted and protected this arrogance among its white players, owners, and fans. As the game became an indispensable part of the nation's daily rhythms, the white middle class accepted a degree of rabidity in its fans and demanded it from its local writers. The result was printed tirades that freely called an umpire a "mutton-headed little freak" and a "contemptible loud-mouthed little chunk of nothing" as well as apocryphal stories like the one in which a boy who has asked his employer for the afternoon off to attend his grandmother's burial is told, "This is the eighth grandmother you have buried since the base ball season opened." The boy replies: "I know it sir; I came of a very old family, and my ancestors can't stand the excitement of two leagues. They're dyin' off fast."[59]

Further, the game's business side did not miss its former Negro players. Black spectators continued to attend professional white games, often acquiescing in the indignity of segregated seating to do so. Only one astute observer, it seemed, noticed the connections between baseball's hypocrisy, its symbolic status as the national pastime, and its implications for defining American character. In a plaintive letter to the *Sporting Life* in March 1888, Weldy Walker, incorrectly anticipating a color line being drawn in the Ohio State League, wrote:

> I am convinced that you all, as a body of men, have not been impartial and unprejudiced in your consideration of the great and important question – the success of the "National game" . . . The law is a disgrace to the present age, and reflects very much upon the intelligence of your last meeting, and casts derision at the laws of Ohio – the voice of the people – that say all men are equal. I would suggest that your honorable body, in case that black law is not repealed, pass one making it criminal for a colored man or woman to be found in a ball ground. There is now the same accommodation made for the colored patron of the game as the white, and the same provision and dispensation is made of the money of them both that finds its way into the coffers of the various clubs.
>
> There should be some broader cause – such as want of ability, behavior, and intelligence – for barring a player than his color. It is for

these reasons and because I think ability and intelligence should be recognized first and last – at all times and by everyone – I ask the question again, why was the "law permitting colored men to sign repealed, etc.?"[60]

It is instructive and perhaps prescient that in his reiteration of qualifications in the closing paragraph, Weldy omitted behavior. Two months later, brother Fleet would stride the Toronto ball grounds with his loaded revolver, aggravating one more white suspicion about Negro fitness for living in an integrated and competitive world. Even so, the strangest note to the end of Fleet Walker as a professional baseball player was that this man, once called one of the finest ballplayers in the nation, could offer little evidence in 1889 against the argument that he had played his way out of the game.

Just how good a professional ballplayer had Moses Fleetwood Walker actually been? If the boxscore has proven to be baseball's guide to twentieth-century talent, it has been no Rosetta stone for deciphering the statistics of players involved in a nineteenth-century game that was changing too quickly to be captured by numbers. Walker's talent can neither be assessed through statistics nor filtered through the yearning hopes of late nineteenth-century sportswriters; they were often too anxious to crusade against the cruelties of society by knighting the symbols of various struggles. Walker was assuredly fast and strong armed. If he never tested himself behind the plate against Cap Anson, he had played against many other major leaguers. He had played against Charles Comiskey and Pete Browning. He once threw out John Montgomery Ward stealing – a rarity. Perhaps it is enough to know that in an age of surging racism where umpires admitted to making calls and teammates admitted to subverting their play on the basis of color, with the alternative of all-Negro teams beckoning, and despite the physical demands on an aging catcher, predominantly white teams in competitive leagues had, for seven years, paid Moses Fleetwood Walker to play baseball. That is how good he was.

Baseball did more for Fleet Walker than provide a paycheck and a chance to prove white men wrong about the physical capacities of blacks, however. The auxiliary aspects of the game – the travel, the press clippings, the fan attention – also flushed from cover some of the personality of Fleet Walker, highlighting his contradictory impulses without distinguishing between the good and the bad. They accentuated his showmanship – he participated in and won pregame throwing contests to great applause. They aggravated his adversarial nature – when denied hotel accommodations, Fleet Walker brought suit. They also exacerbated the darker side – alcohol and weapons became companions.

In 1889, Fleet Walker's time as a touring exhibit expired. A gentleman who supposedly would not go where he was not wanted, he had insisted on seven years in white leagues. For seven years he had been a traveling laboratory rat for the tenets of race theory, required to tailor his public behavior to the tolerance level and expectations of white society. Until the revolver incident in Toronto it had been nearly impossible to know from Walker's public demeanor how deeply men like Cap Anson and those who tried to cast blacks from the International League had cut into his hopes. Not for decades, until the immediacy of the connections had been lost, would it become apparent that the tears in Fleet Walker's divided heart had begun to pull apart in ways that a Wednesday's child could not conceal forever.

Setting aside the victories of Marshall "Major" Taylor, a black cyclist who did much of his racing abroad, a Negro would not serve as a highly visible public exhibit for physical race differences again until after the turn of the century. When he did, it was behind the bars of a cage in New York's Bronx Zoo primate house. By then, the American and National Leagues had stabilized the business of major league baseball. Their annual clash in the glorious fiction of a "World" Series had solidified the game's place in American consciousness. The idea of colored Americans among the sport's playing professionals was a distant memory.

In the decade following his banishment, however, Fleet Walker did not forget. The last photograph of him as a ballplayer, one taken with the 1889 Syracuse Stars, finds him staring past the camera and into the distance, his coal-black eyes seeming to bore through time. While he had grown remarkably handsome, the softness that marks his Oberlin team photo is gone. No, he would not forget. Though, like the exiled Moses, he would temporarily lose the attention that had been his, he would reclaim it in dramatic and unhappy ways.

4

· · · · · · · · · · · · · · · ·

We believe the body we have viewed is that of

Patrick Murray. We find that his death was caused

by hemorrhage from a wound in the abdomen, made

by a knife in the hand of one Moses F. Walker.

Coroner's inquest, April 1891

SUNLIGHT TO DARKNESS

The first biblical portrait of Moses as an adult is that of a killer. Though Egyptians had raised him, when Moses observed one beating a Jew, he struck out in support of a more deeply felt allegiance and killed the Egyptian. Though Moses Fleetwood Walker was thirty-three years old in April 1891, in a sense his adult life was just beginning. His emergence into a world without baseball would elicit from him a response eerily similar to that of Moses. Part white, raised in racially tolerant areas, schooled in assimilationist institutions, and wedged into an exciting, glamorous, overwhelmingly white profession, Fleet Walker had had access to the same sort of illusions that protected Moses as a child. But Moses was a Jew, not an Egyptian, and Walker was a mulatto, not a white. Further, any illusions Walker may have held about race harmony had been steeping in the reality of his baseball trips to the South and his clashes with Cap Anson. Now Northern baseball men had dropped a veil between him and the game with the finality and surprise of a friend's betrayal, and so, in April 1891, Walker found himself moving through the streets of Syracuse, carrying a message, as well as the accumulated bile of his imposed exile.

On Thursday, 9 April, shortly after 1 P.M., Fleet Walker left his home at 338 Green Street to deliver a message in another part of the city. After a number of inquiries he found his destination, dropped the message, and reversed direction for home. A social visit at a saloon lengthened his return trip so that it was not until about 4 P.M. that he reached the corner of Monroe and Orange streets. There he became engaged with a small group of white men. Within several minutes one of the men had a fatal stab wound and Moses Fleetwood Walker lay unconscious in a prison cell, charged with a premeditated and deliberate slaying – murder in the first degree.

In one brief moment made of beer and bad judgment, Moses Fleetwood Walker, the educated, graceful athlete, the player once described in the press as a "perfect gentleman,"[1] again had become a case study for white contentions and fears. He had become the razor-carrying Negro; the temperamental, vengeful mulatto; he had given the many whites who were regarding all persons with a single drop of Negro blood as one undifferentiated dark mass a reason to assert their claims as valid. Less than two years from his baseball retirement, Walker was going back on exhibit as a specimen for race theory, this time for reasons of social rather than physical deportment.

Though Syracuse had just been host to another spectacular murder forty-eight hours earlier, the intrigue and disposition of Fleet Walker's case held new drama. It had all the elements necessary to enlist public interest: overtones of race, class, and celebrity; enough witnesses to hopelessly muddle the truth; the promise of a courtroom trial to re-fashion its ugliness into a coherent allegory of the times; and enough newspaper interest to draw out the seamy details.

The two Syracuse dailies, the *Courier* and the *Daily Journal,* attempted in their day-after editions to frame the apparent facts. These initial accounts, gleaned from conversation with friends of the slain and a policeman, said that a considerably intoxicated Walker had reacted to a comment from one of the group by cursing and insulting the speaker. The deceased, bricklayer Patrick "Curly" Murray, and his cousin, Patrick "Boodle" Murray, responded by approaching Walker while returning the insults. Walker stabbed Curly with a large, two-bladed pocket knife, then started east. The victim picked up a stone from the street and flung it at Walker, but Curly's fading strength left the rock well short of its mark. One of the group left in search of a recently departed foot patrolman, while two others overtook Walker and held him until a patrol wagon arrived and bore him to the police station where he fell into a sleep until 9 P.M. Curly, bleeding from a deep wound that began in the left groin and penetrated upward into the intestines, was carried to the home of an-other cousin. Through the course of the evening, during which Curly remained painfully conscious while continually vomiting blood, the district attorney, three doctors, the coroner, the deputy sheriff, a priest, and several reporters visited the house. Walker, waking later that night in his cell, asked Captain Quigley, "What kind of a chap was that I cut?" Told he was a pretty good fellow, Walker retorted, "Well, he made a bad break when he came for me." Indeed he had. Curly Murray, numbed with morphine injections, remained conscious throughout the night, but died shortly before 3 A.M. in the company of his wife, Kittie, and a doctor.

The *Courier* descriptions of the two principals were flattering to neither. Murray had two prior arrests involving burglary and receiving stolen property. For the second he had served three years in nearby Auburn prison, made famous in 1890 for hosting the nation's first electrocution. At the time of the stabbing, he had been working steadily for a few years and living with Kittie.[2]

It was more important to figure out just what sort of chap the assailant was. Walker, who was according to the *Courier* the "best catcher the Syracuse club ever had," lived with his wife and three children. In a statement that revealed the shortcomings of fame – the inescapable attention that breeds public familiarity and innuendo – the *Courier* said that Walker "is a very intelligent and gentlemanly fellow when sober and good natured but is said to possess a very dangerous temper when aroused or when in drink." Further, the paper claimed that Walker had been fined for once drawing a revolver on a man in Toronto.[3]

Had reporters or policemen recognized the indignity inherent in Walker's forced departure from the International Association, they might have known that his rancor was searching for a target. After the Syracuse Stars cut him during the 1889 season, Walker may have tried to stay in baseball. Later writers claimed that he played with Terre Haute of the Western Association in 1890. He did not. Though Terre Haute's catchers were broken and bruised often, though the team released its first and second string catchers on the same day in July, Fleet Walker never played for the Hautentots. If he even tried out for the team, the local press, which always allotted front page space to the team, never mentioned it. A few histories have also mistakenly claimed that Walker finished play in 1891 in Oconto, Wisconsin. He did not.

If Walker contacted potential teams, his efforts failed. He remained in Syracuse to make a home and a new start. His partnership with the local Syracuse umpire must not have worked out after its promising start, because in 1890 he was again at work for the postal service. With the help of John C. Bowe, druggist, manufacturer, and former director of the Stars, Walker secured a job as a railway mail clerk, handling registered letters on runs between Syracuse and New York City. It was an important, responsible position, but, as before, clearly beneath his talents. It held little possibility for creativity, excitement, drama, fulfillment – in short, it had nothing to offer an ambitious, talented man, particularly one who had already felt celebrity's rush. So it was that Fleet Walker had not gone quietly or exclusively about his clerking business.

Part of his restlessness he turned loose on invention. In the late 1880s a former Syracuse University professor, Dr. Joel Gilbert Justin, had become interested in shooting dynamite artillery shells using conventional gunpowder rather than compressed air. The only problem was that the shells kept blowing apart upon firing. The solution rested in constructing a shell that would hold together until impact with its target. In the spring of 1890 previous experiments left him confident enough in what came to be referred to as the "Justin Gun" to schedule a final demonstration to which he invited prominent engineers, government officials, and a representative of the Chinese government. On 27 May, with an audience of more than a thousand massed on the rim of a deep gorge near Perryville, Justin fired his newly adapted "monster nine-inch Blakely rifle." An instant later the crowd was "dodging flying fragments of iron and steel," all that was left of Justin's years of invention.[4]

Fleet Walker, schooled in the theoretical knowledge of projectiles from the mechanics course of his sophomore year at Oberlin, and in the practicalities of firearms from his revolver-carrying days in Toronto, became intrigued with Justin's failure. By February 1891 he had assigned two-thirds interest in his first invention, a dynamite artillery shell in an ingenious outer casing designed to remedy Justin's failure, to Bowe and to the firm of George Hey, Alfred Wilkinson, and Arthur Parsons, patent attorneys in Syracuse. Their firm had been among a list of baseball ticket holders whose subscriptions would help later that spring to save the fiscally troubled Stars.[5]

Walker invested the invention with hopes for his own financial salvation, believing that there was "a great demand" for such a projectile.[6] That fall the *Cleveland Gazette* reported that he had devised a "cartridge that will do the deadly work claimed for the Justin gun . . . If he has, his fortune is made."[7] In August the U.S. Patent Office granted to Walker, Bowe, and Hey, Wilkinson, and Parsons, patent number 45345 for the guaranteed-to-explode artillery shell, but it did not confirm Fleet's conviction about demand for such a product. In the world of late nineteenth-century invention, the breathtaking pace of new developments often rendered yesterday's ingenuity as obsolete as the wooden club. Within a decade another black, Eugene Burkins, invented a rapid-fire gun that scientific journals pronounced a decided advance in ordnance and gunnery.[8] Unfortunately, Fleet Walker became a public figure in 1891 for his other deadly involvement, the incident at Orange and Monroe streets. Before he could move on to greater things, he had to clear the imposing hurdle of a murder trial.

At issue in the trial was something larger than an argument resolved with a knife: a determination of the source and limits of Fleet Walker's rage. It may have been no greater in 1891 than during any of the past dozen years, but when he allowed it that year to sneak past the well-heeled manners and handsome face and ignite the temper, he lost a treasured and cultivated ally. Anger reduced Fleet Walker's character to ashes. What made this so significant was that in the America of the 1890s, character was literally the last thing a mulatto could afford to lose.

In that decade the determination of whites to merge scientific race theory, economic practicality, and a swelter of amorphous fears into a solid barrier between themselves and Negroes came to fruition. The results would be more visibly depressing in the first decade of the new century, but watching the process unfold was undoubtedly more distressing to blacks. It was the difference between the panic of a tightening lynch noose and the resignation of watching the lifeless corpse swing from a tree.

By 1890 most whites and many blacks had come to accept as genuine the sham of race theorists and their claims of Negro intellectual inferiority. Twisted interpretations of anthropometric measurements reinforced it and predicted its inevitable and perpetual continuance. Claims of physical inferiority were more problematic. Still, the evidence of black susceptibility to disease, not to mention continuing claims of mulatto sterility, underscored white hopes for black extinction. When a black like Fleet Walker had insisted on parading his physical talents on a ball field, official policy and studied ignorance had stripped him bare. Out of sight, out of contention. Social equality thus became the last open avenue for blacks still hopeful in 1890 of securing a place in American culture. Of course, it was the realm that white bigots were least willing to cede, but segments of the black population were intent on exhibiting character and comportment, of proving to white society that blacks had the grace to warrant approval if not admiration.

Clinging most tightly to the hope for elevation through respectability, education, social grace, and moral rectitude was a "colored aristocracy" that had existed at least since the 1830s. Among this small group at the top of Negro society, ancestry and light color were the seeds of status. Self-restraint, the prime attribute of gentility, could nurture the seeds. The black aristocrats believed the crudities and vulgarities of the colored masses were responsible for a great deal of white discrimination. Many argued for ostracism of the "prostitutes, thieves, loafers, and other 'vicious' elements of the race."[9] Unfortunately, their insistence on proper behavior only bolstered white claims that race relations would be best served if Negroes peacefully and passively accepted a subordinate place.

Though nearly all Americans near the century's close assumed that proper conduct indicated proper character, many whites found the notion of a black elite laughable. In fact, they were ready to put an end to the perceived nonsense of accrediting mulattos, quadroons, and octoroons as slivers of the white population. Sorting out heritage based on skin shading was inexact work at best, and in the 1890s the wrangling over fractional definitions lessened. It was far easier to consider the whole mass of black-tinged people as just plain Negroes. Henceforth, one drop of black blood would suffice to make a person black.

This notorious "one-drop rule," widely accepted in white America by 1915, cast a damning light on race mixture and dulled the hopes of light-skinned Negro aristocrats who saw themselves as uniquely capable of building a bridge between the races.[10] A rising number of lynchings since 1885 – up to 192 in 1891, 235 in 1892[11] – and attempts to legally disenfranchise blacks revealed a white yearning for gulfs, not bridges. Though often dressed in articulate argument, at the heart of the yearning was a primal white fear that American blacks might revert to their primitive African roots.

Ironically, back-to-Africa schemes became cause for heated debate among blacks at this time. Though they were proposed as opportunities to establish advanced Negro cultures, suggestions of an African return in fact contributed to the notions of irreversible racial essences and differences. Race scientists continued to promote these notions, arguing that even in mulattos basic Negro characteristics remained, "lurking beneath the surface of white skin and straight hair," ready to reappear at any time in an atavistic child.[12] The inferiority lurked, of course, in the blood. Even some blacks believed that those of the race who were backward and degraded were the result of inferior blood.[13] One drop of the wrong blood, then, could undo an otherwise cultured individual, return him to the law of the jungle.

That someone as cultured, refined, and dignified as Fleet Walker may have made the leap backward was, then, an important matter to settle. Interestingly, the black press, though it would later defend Walker, was not initially unequivocal. The *Cleveland Gazette* thought it evident that Walker had killed in self-defense after being insulted, but it also reported that he had "dropped into a drunken stupor after his arrest."[14]

Oberlin College's first varsity nine, 1881. *Top row* (left to right): Julian C. Moore, Charles D. Harrison, Weldy W. Walker, Merton E. Thompson. *Middle row:* Moses Fleetwood Walker, Josiah H. Bellows, Willis F. Day, Edward B. Burwell. *Bottom:* Charles D. Green, Harlan F. Burket, Arthur T. Packard. Both Walkers, Burket, and Burwell would play professionally. Note the mask perched atop Fleet's left knee and the cumbersome shoes. Courtesy Oberlin College Archives.

A scoresheet from the 1881 season, likely from the book Julian Moore clutches in the team photo. On this day Weldy assumed an uncommon role, outperforming his big brother. Courtesy Oberlin College Archives.

Tappan Square, Oberlin College, ca. 1875. There is a baseball diamond in the right foreground. Later the field was moved, allowing Fleet Walker to strike his legendary blow over Cabinet Hall, which is the white building on the far right in the distance. Courtesy Oberlin College Archives.

Weldy Walker, *front row center,* with the 1883 University of Michigan baseball team. Courtesy Bentley Historical Library, University of Michigan.

Moses Fleetwood Walker, catcher for Toledo of the Northwestern League,
1883. Courtesy National Baseball Library and Archive, Cooperstown NY.

OLIN LANE WELCH BARKLEY MULLANE O'DAY MEISTER POORMAN
MILLER MORTON McGUIRE ARUNDEL

(*Above*) Toledo Blue Stockings, Northwestern League champions, 1883. M. F. Walker is *back row center.* Courtesy Jerry Malloy.

(*Below*) The major league Toledo squad of 1884. An old caption noted that "Moses Fleetwood Walker – (Colored Catcher) was absent when the picture was taken," a circumstance that likely pleased bigoted teammates Tony Mullane and Curt Welch. Manager Morton is seated in center. Future umpire Hank O'Day is in *back row,* and "Deacon" McGuire, Walker's replacement, is stretched out in the *right front.* Courtesy Jerry Malloy.

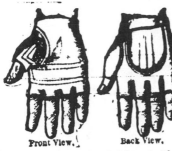

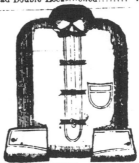
A J. D. Shibe Company ad from 1884 shows the type of padded leather gloves
that Walker occasionally used as well as the latest in catchers' masks.

The 1888 White Stockings. Duval, the mascot, is in *center.* Cap Anson, Walker's bane, stands directly behind Duval. On Anson's right is Fred "Fritz" Pfeffer, one of the ballplayers who stalked off the field when Walker appeared ready to enter an 1881 contest in Louisville. Courtesy National Baseball Library and Archive, Cooperstown NY.

The Syracuse Stars, 1888 champions of the International Association. Fleet Walker is at *far left of top row.* Pitcher Robert Higgins is seated *at left.* Courtesy National Baseball Library and Archive, Cooperstown NY.

M. F. WALKER.
CARTRIDGE.

No. 458,026.
Patented Aug. 18, 1891.

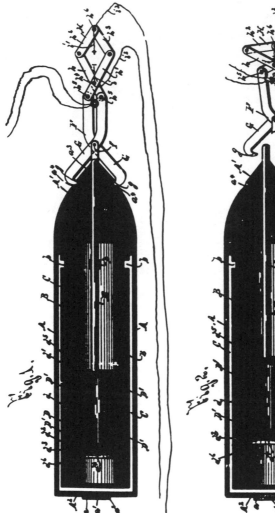

WITNESSES:

INVENTOR
Moses F. Walker

BY
ATTORNEYS

The patent drawing for M. F. Walker's 1891 invention,
the exploding artillery shell.

Opposite the Court House in Cadiz, Ohio ca. 1910. Fleet and Ednah Walker's
Opera House is the second building from the left (the Court House statue
appears to be almost touching it). Courtesy Harrison County Historical
Society.

The Cadiz Opera House, one-quarter century after Fleet Walker's death, had been converted to other purposes. Courtesy Harrison County Historical Society.

Whether or not that was true, the morning after the assault, 10 April, found Walker standing "neatly dressed and self-composed" for arraignment in police court. Evincing his familiarity with the law and the gravity of his situation, he had shrewdly arranged already for counsel.[15] Casting his eyes over Walker, Justice Mulholland, in another affirmation of Walker's celebrity, sadly shook his head and sighed, "Moses, Moses, Moses." In answer to routine questions, Walker gave his age as thirty-two, and admitted to a prior conviction. His attorney, Harrison Hoyt, asked that Walker be committed to the penitentiary to await the grand jury. He was taken there in the afternoon.[16]

Following the arraignment, Walker gave a *Courier* reporter his version of the incident: a saloonkeeper who knew him as a ballplayer had interrupted his walk home, inviting him inside for three beers and a talk about baseball. He was not, he said, intoxicated in the least. When he later passed Murray's group, one of them shouted: "What is the son of a —— of a nigger doing down this way?" (The *Courier* obviously regarded some other word as more offensive to its readers than *nigger*). In a revealing reply, Walker showed how precariously he was perched atop the fence separating docility from aggression. He told them that he was "minding his own business" and that "he had as much of a right there as they did." He then crossed the street and "was going on without saying a word." At that point, a rock struck him in the back of the head, cutting through his hat and raising a lump on the back of his head. Here Walker showed a half-dollar-sized swelling to the reporter and then exhibited his derby, which was cut through the band and the felt. "If it was not for the thickness of my hat, I think it would have killed me," he said. "My first thought was to find a stone to throw back. I began to hunt for one, but the blow so dazed and bewildered me that I could see nothing. Then I remembered that they crowded around me and I was afraid that I would be struck again."[17]

The first official testimony came the next day, 11 April, at the coroner's inquest, and it became evident that a jury was going to have a number of stories from which to choose. Boodle Murray was present, but did not testify, the prosecution electing to reserve his account for a later trial. Among others, four eyewitnesses took the stand, however, and refuted Walker's claims. They all asserted that Walker had chased Murray. One, John Curtain, probably lost his chance to testify at a later trial when he claimed that he saw Walker chase Murray, but also said he saw Murray hit Walker in the back of the head with something, an interesting feat for a man being pursued.[18] Whatever consistency the stories of the four may have had stemmed from their agreement in this: there were angry words exchanged before the stabbing, and the insults dealt with character.

Whether intentional or not, the confrontation gave substance to the ongoing struggle of Irish and blacks to avoid the bottom rung of society's ladder. The Irish turned out in large numbers the next day, 12 April, to bury Curly Murray. Following a funeral mass at Saint Patrick's Church, six pallbearers from Murray's bricklayers union, whose members attended en masse, lowered their former workmate to his grave.[19] Fleet Walker awaited his own fate in the penitentiary.

He waited nearly a month. The grand jury did not convene until 8 May. Walker's case was heard after the indictment of Antonio Glielmi for first-degree murder. Glielmi had shot a man in Syracuse's Clinton Square less than two days before Walker stabbed Murray. In the month between arrest and trial, the charge against Walker had been reduced to second-degree murder. Asked his plea, Walker replied with wavering voice, "Not guilty." He was indicted nonetheless.[20]

During May, as Moses Fleetwood Walker again waited in jail, this time for his jury trial, Thomas Edison gave the first public showing of a motion picture. In later years, filmmakers would repeatedly exploit the drama of murder trials. Their work – framing angles, highlighting pathos, elevating performance – complements that of trial attorneys perfectly. The Walker contest would have been a fitting subject for rolling cameras. When Fleet was led into the courtroom on 1 June, a quirk in American society, and consequently American jurisprudence, became obvious: facts are just one part of perceived reality; performance is equally weighty. Later in life, Fleet would understand the importance of this truism to the cinema. It was clear from the trial's outset that he and his attorneys already had a grasp of its significance in the courtroom.

When the assistant district attorney, a man appropriately named Shove, opened the trial on 1 June with a graphic description of the stabbing and a portrayal of Curly Murray as a peaceful man whose approach to Walker with outstretched hand had been one of conciliation, Fleet and Arabella Walker countered with tears and drawn handkerchiefs. In fact, Bella held her husband's hand throughout the trial, her devotion and beauty entrusted to leave their subtle marks on the jury. The twelve jurors were all men, all white. Eight were farmers. A gardener, a tobacco dealer, an agent, and a cooper (Moses W. Walker's onetime occupation) completed the panel. They could not have been oblivious to this "very good looking young woman," misjudged by a reporter to be twenty-three or twenty-four years old, who looked "more like a dark brunett than a colored woman."[21] As long as the jurors did not mistake her for white, Bella Walker's good looks would enhance perceptions of her husband's civility and character.

She was just one of the aspects that loomed favorably for Walker. Harrison Hoyt was another. He had a reputation as a skilled advocate, and he was joined by an assistant, M. Z. Haven. The defense team's third attorney was A. C. Lewis, Fleet's former mentor, who had traveled from Steubenville to be at the accused's side. All members of the defense team were white.[22] And then there was, of course, Walker himself. As always, his dress and carriage were impeccably appropriate. Additionally, he had an understanding of the law and experience in a courtroom. The *Cleveland Gazette* claimed that Walker had been recently admitted to the bar in Toledo. Though he had actually never even sat for the entrance exam, he was nonetheless better prepared than the average murder defendant for the combat of trial.[23]

Allegiances of the press and public were uncertain. Following the indictment, the *Courier* had reported the next day that the bill was against Moses *T.* Walker, the colored *pugilist*. It was one of many small discrepancies that foreshadowed the trial coverage ahead. The *Courier* would be slightly more sympathetic to the dead Murray, the *Daily Journal* would lean slightly towards Walker. Interestingly, neither paper showed an inclination for the racial innuendo accorded Glielmi (the Italian indicted for murder the same day as Walker). According to the *Daily Journal,* Glielmi's response to his first grand jury question had been, "I no-a understand."[24]

The crowd that filled the courtroom and spilled into adjoining hallways during the trial attested only that Walker was a figure of public interest. Whether they viewed Walker as a sympathetic figure – a popular former ballplayer squeezed out of his profession by discrimination – or as a celebrity felon, their loyalties would not become clear until the verdict was announced.

The eyewitnesses who would testify against Walker were unquestionably biased. The prosecution sought to build a sympathetic foundation for them by first calling to the stand the seemingly neutral voice of authority, arresting policeman Frank A. Sheriff. Sheriff testified that he had known the victim for about ten years. His beat had carried him on the afternoon of 9 April to the corner of Orange and Monroe where a group of four men, including the two Murrays, sat on the steps of a saloon. Walker was also there, standing on the other edge of the sidewalk. As he passed time among the group, Sheriff heard Walker say, "They are bad people around here," and heard someone else reply, "No, I guess not." Here, Sheriff remarked, "I thought Walker was intoxicated." The patrolman continued on his way, but a small boy soon summoned him back. Returning to the corner, the officer noted that,

"Everything was in a hurly burly . . . The men were running in all directions and yelling that Walker had stabbed Murray." He saw four men carrying the body of another. He saw Richard Barry and Anthony McNamara talking to Walker at the corner of Monroe and Almond. He arrested the compliant Walker and began escorting him to the station. They had gone a short distance when a boy shouted, "He has dropped his knife." Sheriff told the boy to keep it until he came back. On the way to the station, Sheriff said he asked Walker, "Why did you not go on and not meddle with that crowd?" Walker's answer, he claimed, was, "Why, I could clean that whole crowd out."

During cross-examination, Harrison Hoyt challenged Sheriff's ability to judge Walker as intoxicated. Pressed, the policeman could give no symptoms of drunkenness other than a "general look." But, reasoned Hoyt, "this man's face is quite dark." Sheriff could offer no better description. "He looked," he asserted, "a little dull." Sheriff, in fact, had previously told the grand jury that Walker did not appear to be drunk until they were nearly to the station.[25] Hoyt asked if Sheriff thought Boodle Murray had also been drunk.

"It would be a hard thing to tell when Boodle Murray was drunk."

"He was in his normal condition when drunk, was he?"

"If Boodle Murray was found lying down and unable to get up it would be safe to conclude that he was drunk."

The next witness, Josiah B. Morgan, another police officer, attested that Walker had arrived at the station drunk. Charles Wright, Chief of Police, then identified the knife, acknowledged that the police had several photos of the five-feet-eight-inch, one-hundred-sixty-pound Murray, and testified that he had seen a "bunch" on the back of Walker's head and a crack in Walker's hat the day after the killing.

As the first day drew to a close, the prosecution finished with an emotional flourish. Among the last to be called, Captain Quigley reiterated the dialogue of his prison cell chat with Walker though the pressure of being under oath transformed his previous assessment of Murray as a "pretty good fellow" into one in which the bricklayer became "not a Sunday School teacher." Next, Dr. D. M. Totman described Murray's wounds, his uninterrupted bleeding, and recited the dying man's contentions that "a man named Walker stabbed me. I gave him no provocation." The deathbed confession might have sounded as flat and insincere as it likely was had not the prosecution decided to vivify it with an electrifying piece of courtroom theatrics. The assistant undertaker took the stand following Totman, and brought with him the gruesome spectacle of Murray's bloody clothing. If it affected the jury as deeply as it did

Bella Walker, Fleet Walker was in trouble; as he left the courtroom, his unnerved wife remained behind to weep openly.[26]

The next morning, the defense struck back. When Walker came up from the cell, one of his young sons presented him with a handful of flowers. As the boy sat next to him with his head occasionally resting on his father's shoulder, Fleet patted his hand. Again, Bella held her husband's hand throughout the day. The touching family portrait robbed impact from the testimony of the day's opening witness, Richard Barry.

Barry was building a cellar on Monroe Street on 9 April. When he first saw an acquaintance, Curly Murray, Murray's hand was covering his left side, and he was trying to pick something up and throw it. Murray told Barry he had been stabbed. Barry said he then noticed Walker following Curly, and Boodle Murray following Walker. Walker carried a knife and, according to Barry, told him he intended to kill Curly. Barry said that he then leaped from the cellar and wrested the knife from Walker, who left, went a short way, and then returned and demanded the knife. Afraid that Walker's motion toward a hip pocket and his threat to "load" Barry might signal possession of a gun, Barry returned the knife, and Walker again started away. He came back once more when Barry called after him, offering to buy him a drink and showing him the silver coins to do so. He then distracted Walker with conversation until the police arrived. Hoyt's cross-examination explored some contradictions, but did not shake the core of Barry's testimony.

The next several witnesses added little, though a woman who lived across the street from Crouse's saloon said that when she first saw Walker, he had crossed the street to shake hands with one of the Irish group, "Tailor" McNamara. Testimony then came from three more of Murray's acquaintances. Among other things, they claimed that Walker was intoxicated, that he had opened first the smaller and then the larger blade of his knife, that the argument between Walker and the Murrays concerned their relative abilities to be trusted for more drinks, and that Curly had thrown the stone at Walker after being stabbed. Hoyt extracted from the last of these men an admission that both Murrays were advancing on Walker at the time of the stabbing, and that Walker had moved about seven feet away from the sidewalk before their approach.

The prosecution's case closed with Tailor McNamara. His account was less lopsided than those that had come before. It seemed he knew Walker. He said, in fact, that he had met him earlier in the day for a beer. He insisted, under cross-examination, that Walker was drunk, his drooped eyes giving him a "dozy" look. McNamara also insisted that the argument was about beer. Before the stabbing, he had walked into the street with Walker and asked him to put away his knife. He saw both Murrays pick up stones, but did not see Walker hit with one.

Tailor McNamara's father, Anthony, surprisingly was one of the first two witnesses for the defense. He had appeared near Crouse's saloon to admonish his son "to go and do what I had told him." Walker was with his son's group, his foot on the steps. Suddenly, all jumped up but one. The Murrays left and returned quickly with "missiles." They advanced on Walker, Curly swiping at and trying to kick him. Walker warned Curly he would "probe" him if he did not stay back. Finally, Walker lunged at Murray, who immediately put his hand to his side and walked away. According to McNamara, no stones hit Walker before the stabbing. As to the crucial question of Walker's intoxication, McNamara said, "I wouldn't call him drunk, nor I wouldn't call him sober. He was about half and half." At this, the courtroom spectators erupted in laughter, giving evidence that they had not lost sight of Walker's complexion. The judge's gavel was required to restore order, after which McNamara continued. Walker "was a little nervous and a little rough. He did not stagger. He looked like a man who had been on a spree."

Perhaps thinking that McNamara's account had done more damage than good, Hoyt opted next for the drama of Walker's version. In a quiet manner, the defendant detailed his movements of 9 April. As reconstructed by the two daily papers, his story was essentially this: he had gone that afternoon in search of Joseph Simmons, onetime manager of the Syracuse Stars, for whom he had a message related to baseball matters in Waterbury, Connecticut. On his way back, he stopped at O'Brien's saloon for "three or four small glasses of lager beer." He arrived at Orange and Monroe about 4 P.M. Walker recollected seeing several men on Crouse's saloon steps. One said, "There comes Walker." Another said, "Hello, Walker." A conversation on baseball matters ensued. When it lagged, Walker said, "I started away. Someone said 'Ain't you going to do something?' I said 'No, I guess not to-day.' Somebody said, 'We can buy our own beer,' and that 'You are putting on a good many airs for a d——— nigger.' I said that it did not cost them anything; that I did not stop to quarrel with them, and that it was not necessary for them to insult me." Walker said he started away when he was struck in the back of the head with a stone. "I turned around," he said next, "thinking to pick up a stone, but I did not see one and one of the party was so close to me that I did not have time to look for one." Neglecting to note that he had found time to draw his knife, Walker continued his story. One of the men had approached Walker. When the man struck at him, Walker dodged him and threw out his hand. "Then," the witness asserted, "others came for me and I heard one say 'Kick the d——d nigger's head off.' "

"Did you call any of them Irish —— ——?" asked Hoyt.

"No, but I believe I said when I turned to go away, in reply to something, 'None of your business, you dirty loafers.' After I was hit by the stone my sight was affected. I saw stars and could not distinguish one person from another. I have no recollection of chasing Murray around the cellar."

On cross-examination, Walker said he had looked in three or four saloons for Simmons, but entered none. He admitted that he frequently drank beer, but said he did not get drunk. He also admitted that he had told Sheriff that the group was "a pretty bad crowd, but only in a joke. I had no motive for it at that time." He had a faint recollection of his arrest, but none of dropping his knife.

Asked if he had ever previously drawn a weapon, Walker said this was the first time. But, asked the prosecutor, hadn't he assaulted a Syracuse neighbor with a hatchet? No, replied Walker, the assault had been on him, and he had had the neighbor arrested. The prosecution was clearly after something. "Did you ever draw a revolver in Toronto on a man?" asked the District Attorney.

"No, sir."

"Or in Detroit?"

"No, sir. I never had a quarrel in Detroit."

"Are you not a violent tempered man?"

"I was never suspected of it."

The district attorney pressed him no further, a stunning surprise since Walker had admitted to a previous conviction in police court and since the prosecution obviously had some idea that the conviction revolved around the incident that had taken place at the Toronto ballpark. Amazingly, at the time of the incident in 1888, either as a measure of Walker's popularity, or as an attempt to mute racial overtones that might have accrued to the incident, the *Syracuse Daily Courier* had never mentioned the revolver affair in its coverage of the Stars. It had merely reported the Stars' win. At Walker's trial, then, the necessary details of the affair were apparently unknown to the prosecution. Thus when Walker answered that he had not *drawn* a revolver, he was quite possibly telling the truth. When the prosecution's incomplete knowledge turned their inquiry mistakenly to Detroit, Walker was probably quite pleased to have them fishing in the wrong waters. Hoyt, on redirect examination, clarified that Walker carried a knife to cut twine on his mail car; he then finished the day by calling five character witnesses in Walker's behalf.[27]

The trial concluded on 3 June. For the final day, Walker brought with him his wife and his mother-in-law. All three children, "well dressed . . . and very light of color for their race," stood by the ladies. The oldest, daughter Cleodolinda, alternated time in Fleet's lap with the youngest boy, George, who had again brought his father a bouquet of flowers. It made, according to the *Courier,* a "domestic picture seldom seen in criminal court," an appearance of "good looks, intelligence, and considerable refinement" that "one might hate to break."

Hoyt sought to supplement the growing sympathy of the still-large crowd by establishing that a blow to the head from a rock might have caused Walker to appear intoxicated and might have caused him to lose the memory of his pursuit of Murray around the cellar. He called two doctors to fortify this position. However, under the district attorney's cross-examination, the second of these defensively argued that an injured man might go on performing certain actions in an unconscious state. Further, he might, after he realized what he had done in an unconscious condition, take steps to conceal the evidence of his crime. The prosecution recalled Dr. Totman to express his belief that while such a paralyzing blow could rob a man of his conscious purpose, that had not been the case with Walker. With that, the evidence was closed. Boodle Murray and others who had testified at the coroner's inquest had never been called. Harrison Hoyt made dramatic note of this in the impassioned summation that followed.

Hoyt's closing address was so eloquent that Fleet and his family burst into tears several times during its delivery. The attorney conceded the stabbing, but accused the prosecution of presenting an inflammatory, unsubstantiated case. Of Shove, Hoyt said, "I have heard that the good die young, and if that be so, my friend, the assistant district attorney, has earned the longest life that I know of." In addition to pointing out the obvious reason for Boodle's absence, Hoyt impugned the other witnesses as "snakes, lizards, pickpockets, and burglars," and observed that not a single witness had claimed to have smelled liquor on the defendant. His two-hour oration was encapsulated in his charge that "the prosecution always loves knives, and weapons, and dead men's clothes when they have no evidence."

It fell to District Attorney T. E. Hancock to try to neutralize Hoyt's powerful rhetoric. He had seen the jurors' eyes well up at the sight of the children so he began by commiserating with the jury's natural sympathy for the Walker family. "It is perfectly proper for them to be there," he admitted, "but this is a case, not of mercies, but of stern duty. I might place another family group at the other end of the table. It would be in widow's weeds." He then turned his attention on Walker: "Gentlemen, if the stories told by murderers were true, not one would ever have been convicted in this court house. You must remember that Walker, college graduate that he is, will tell just as plausible a story as ever has been told." It was no crime, he continued, for a man to get drunk. But no man had a right to drink "who pours down liquid damnation." Next followed a startling statement that condemned Walker the drinker, but also, perhaps unwittingly, Walker the mulatto. Hancock said, "If Walker, with his peculiar constitution and the blood that flows in his veins, is put in such state that he magnifies every trivial incident into a cause for crime, he had no right to touch the stuff." Hancock maintained that Walker, regardless of condition, had miraculously been able to recall everything in his favor, while forgetting everything that militated against him; he remembered, though dazed at the time, that the men had declared "kick the d——d nigger's head off," yet he forgot entirely that he had chased Curly Murray around the cellar wall. As Walker intently watched Hancock sum up, his young son lay asleep in his arms, while Cleodolinda, frightened by Hancock's attack, wept several times.

Finally, Judge Kennedy instructed the jury. He read the statutory definitions for murder in the second degree, manslaughter, and justifiable homicide. His words were favorable to Walker. In some instances, he used actual case circumstances to clarify meanings, explaining, for example, that a large stone could suffice as a threatening weapon and that the jurors must consider whether a blow to the head could confuse a man to the extent that he could not be held responsible for his actions. Kennedy concluded at 5:15 with the warning that it was better that a criminal escape punishment than an innocent man be punished.[28]

At 7:55 P.M. the jury returned. Eight of the twelve had voted to acquit on the first ballot, then had used the next two hours to persuade the reluctant four. Two unexpected occurrences accompanied their verdict of not guilty. First, as the foreman announced Walker's freedom, the large crowd exploded into spontaneous celebration, the courtroom's solemnity giving way to the "hilarity and din of a base-ball field."[29] Kennedy pounded his gavel so hard that the head flew off. He rose and ordered the court sheriff to arrest a half-dozen of the rowdy spectators. When decorum was restored, the second unexpected event occurred. The jury requested that Kennedy give Walker some advice to guide his future behavior. The judge assented. He warned Walker that if he had been in the habit of drinking, that this would mark a "proper time to break off, and hereafter lead a good life." Walker bowed and sat down beside his joyously weeping wife.

Hearty thanks and good feeling pervaded the courtroom. Hoyt escorted Bella to the bench to shake hands and exchange pleasantries with Kennedy. For some minutes Walker was kept busy by well-wishers before he swept Bella out a side door and home, curiously avoiding the large crowd out front.[30]

The trial and the celebration that followed were huge testaments to Fleet Walker's popularity. In their absence, there was nothing extraordinary to suggest that the city felt about or dealt with race in ways different from other American cities, though the number of blacks was small, Walker being just one of only 867 blacks living among Syracuse's 88,000 residents.[31] Certainly the emphasis in the trial on issues of character revealed a shared understanding of its paramount significance to a man's reputation. It took a powerful presence, then, to overcome all that the testimony had uncovered – the contentiousness, the selective memory, the innuendo of hatchets and revolvers, the rumors of bad temper, the reality of a double-bladed knife, the affinity for alcohol. Indeed, this last had been of obvious concern to the jury. The use of alcohol, before it acquired its twentieth-century patina of chemical instability and its status as a collective social disease, was considered to be a matter of individual fallibility, of willpower and character.

Had this trial revealed anything of Fleet Walker's character? The *Cleveland Gazette* shortsightedly dubbed Walker "a hero."[32] It may have been a triumphant moment of sorts, but not a heroic one. Possibly it was a cathartic and sobering experience, though whatever warnings may have attached to the verdict, they did not settle permanently into Walker's psyche. He was momentarily free of jail, but he was not yet free of the character question. Still in front of Walker was the larger part of a decade during which the fortunes and futures of blacks would continue to sink. They had already begun to founder at Oberlin College, where a month before Fleet's trial six black students had caused a scandal when the lady principal had discovered them paired off in separate rooms in a vacant house outside of town. The *Cleveland Gazette,* one of the Negro publications that promoted good character as a ladder for black hopes, opposed the prevailing black sentiment which suspected the college of overreaction. The *Gazette* labeled the students wrong and the whole affair "disgraceful."[33] Walker would find enough disgrace in the 1890s to match that of the Oberlinians and enough despair to keep pace with that of the larger black population.

In 1891 Moses Fleetwood Walker, assuredly now a man devoid of any remnants of youthful innocence, left Syracuse, troubled with the perceived failings of the white race and now burdened with the public revelations of his own weaknesses. He sought to quiet his heart's misgivings by returning to that area of eastern Ohio which had once boasted a reputation for racial tolerance – home to Steubenville. He tried to settle into unremarkable circumstances, the unlikeliest of all possibilities for a remarkable man.

What remained of the Walker family awaited him in Steubenville. Long before Fleet had become an Oberlin student, Cadwallader had departed. The adopted children, Charles and Mary, may have been close by, but like Cadwallader and Lizzie they took a path irrecoverable to history. Those who were left would not always bring ease or stability to Fleet's life, or augur well for his ability to heed the advice of the Syracuse jury. Sister Mary had married John Alexander, a saloonkeeper.[34] William, Fleet's older brother, was still running a saloon, restaurant, and barbershop on Market Street. William was employing another brother as a bartender: Weldy, who after leaving Michigan's homeopathic school, had kicked around in lower levels of professional baseball before returning home.[35]

Whatever encouragement his father might have been able to offer was lost. Scarcely two weeks after Fleet's acquittal for murder, Moses W. Walker died. Whatever counsel he might have passed to his son for new beginnings had evaporated, however, a few years earlier when Moses had separated from Caroline and his Steubenville family and moved to Detroit, where he died.[36] Caroline subsequently shared her home on South Street with her daughter, Sarah, and her daughter's new husband, Simon Merriman, a black Steubenville farm hand, originally from Washington County, Pennsylvania. Merriman had served three years in a Pennsylvania regiment during the Civil War. He would later become Steubenville's first black police officer. The couple wed in 1892.[37]

In that year Fleet chose to again become a railway clerk for the U.S. Post Office, this time at the Wellsville and Bellaire Railroad Post Office, handling letters for the Cleveland and Pittsburg Railroad. As in Syracuse, he handled registered letters, a position of responsibility. He also became involved with Wellsville's Twin City Lodge of the Knights of Pythias, a secret fraternal society not unlike the Masons. The societies were middle-class attempts to create hierarchies within the population, to distinguish through manners, class, and exclusion a better type of person. Within a short time, Walker had risen to the office of "Grand Outer Guard."[38]

Two weeks before Christmas of 1893, Fleet's mother, Caroline, died at age seventy-one of a throat disease.[39] Both parents were thus lost in less than two years. The impact of their deaths, while it may have been great, paled next to that of the one just ahead. On 12 June 1895, after thirty-two years, four months, and twelve days among the living, Arabella Taylor Walker, Fleet's wife and Oberlin sweetheart, succumbed to cancer.[40] She was buried in Steubenville's Union Cemetery, leaving behind three children to be raised by a husband who spent a great deal of time traveling the rails.

In 1898 Oberlin College once again offered up a former classmate as Fleet's wife: Ednah Jane Mason. Ednah had been born in Albany, Ohio, in 1861, a late addition to the large household of her mulatto parents. Her father, Pat, a wagonmaker and repairer, was fifty-five at the time of her birth, and her mother, Catherine, already forty-one. Early in Ednah's childhood the family moved to Oberlin. She graduated from Oberlin High School in 1878, and six years later had her diploma from Oberlin College. She made immediate use of the degree by teaching school at Owensboro, Kentucky. By 1887 she had relocated to Chicago and had begun operating a grocery store and meat market. In 1888 she married William George Price. She stayed in Chicago until 1897; her marriage had ended sometime previously by death or divorce, and she moved home to Oberlin and lived with her parents there for a year. An amiable, intelligent woman, she became the second woman of surpassing beauty and nearly white skin to marry Fleet Walker. Her pretty, straight hair led some who saw her to speculate that she was a product of partially American Indian blood.[41] Whatever her expectations may have been for her life with Fleet, she could not have predicted the challenge that befell her suddenly on 19 September 1898, just four months into her second marriage.

On that date Fleet Walker was again arrested. This time the command to apprehend went to a U.S. Marshal in the name of the President of the United States of America. This time the judicial web would be spun more tightly. Mail robbery was no trifling offense. A jury of ordinary men might let go a killing, a panicked and necessary defense of oneself. The government was not as inclined to regard calculated theft with the same compassion.

For three years a frequent loss of mail had plagued various railway lines in the eastern portion of Ohio, inciting a number of unpleasant confrontations between clerks and postmasters. Among all the affected lines and clerks, investigation showed that Moses F. Walker was the only employee that had regularly sustained the loss of letters he had directly received, with no claim of dispatch to other lines or destinations. When questioned, Walker would readily admit receipt, but deny all knowledge of disposition. So many of these occurred, and "were paid for so cheerfully," that suspicion arose among investigators that Walker "might be borrowing the money from these letters to relieve urgent personal needs."[42]

Two postal inspectors, A. R. Holmes and A. P. Owen, decided to lay a trap; in their jargon, "we placed a registered test on Walker." On 16 September they dropped a registered letter containing seven dollars into a tie-sack headed for Wellsville, Ohio. When it arrived there, Fleet Walker should have delivered it, along with his others, to his connecting clerk. The snare went awry when the connecting clerk, Hugh Montgomery, recognized Inspector Owen waiting for Walker's train on the station platform. As Walker delivered his registers, Montgomery tipped him off to Owen. Walker at once returned to his railcar, and a short time later brought to Montgomery the planted letter. The envelope was torn open, and it now carried the endorsement, "Received in bad order."[43]

Owen and Holmes secured a warrant and arrested Fleet Walker at Bellaire, Ohio, on 19 September. Walker did not resort to forgetfulness as an excuse as the inspectors anticipated. Rather, he remarkably claimed that the letter had been delivered with all his others. Brought before a commissioner of the U.S. District Court in Steubenville on that day, Walker pleaded not guilty. When he could not post bond of fifteen hundred dollars, he went to the Jefferson County jail to await a hearing on 26 September. Apparently, between arrest and hearing, Walker spoke with the press. The *Steubenville Herald-Star* reported that the envelope had been found in Walker's wastebasket in the railcar, but it also explained that messengers dumped the contents of tie-sacks on a table in the car. The sacks were never used for registered letters. Therefore, the paper said, when Walker noted the letter in the tie-sack, he at once concluded that it had gone astray and had appropriated it.[44]

The *Steubenville Weekly Gazette* sprang to Walker's defense. Citing his monthly salary of eighty dollars and his single daily run between Wellsville and Bellaire, the paper asked, "Is it reasonable to assume his guilt?" If he opened letters and abstracted money, it further mused, would he leave a "tell-tale envelope in his waste basket?"[45]

When Walker appeared for his hearing, he had two attorneys, John M. Cook and John McClave, both of Steubenville. His old friend, A. C. Lewis, was now a prosecuting attorney, but he no doubt had a part in arranging for Walker's case to be handled by McClave, his former partner. Rees G. Richards, the U.S. Commissioner, heard just four witnesses, including both inspectors and Montgomery. Though Holmes testified that despite the envelope's torn condition, the letter, cards, and money had not been removed, and though the defense implied that the inspectors themselves had enlarged the tear in the envelope used as evidence, Richards was convinced that there was probable cause to hold Walker for a December grand jury session. He agreed to lower bail to one thousand dollars. Walker, still unable to pay, remained in the county jail.[46]

In the next month the *Weekly Gazette* continued to support Walker by ridiculing the merits of the government charges. In the first week of October, the paper asserted that the case "grows weaker every day," giving Walker's "legion" of friends cause to "breathe easy once more." At month's end, the paper openly declared that Steubenville's colored voters were convinced the case was "some sinister design . . . to trip up Fleet Walker." They believed that a recent trap laid for another black mail agent warranted their suspicion of racial motives.[47]

Finally, on 24 October, Walker reappeared in front of the commissioner, now able to meet bail. He was not alone. Three friends became jointly indebted to attain Walker's freedom. Among them was Fleet's brother-in-law, Simon Merriman. Given the difficulty of amassing the bond amount, the earlier speculation of Holmes and Owen that Walker needed stolen cash to relieve urgent personal needs seemed credible. It gained further weight when Walker went before a grand jury in Columbus in December without his Steubenville attorneys. Despite his salary, on 9 December, Walker had filed an affidavit as an indigent prisoner. The court appointed a Columbus lawyer to handle his defense. At Walker's request, the court summoned four witnesses in behalf of his "good character": a Steubenville friend, a Bellaire druggist, an acquaintance from the Columbus office of the *Ohio State Journal,* and the Wellsville postmaster. The last of these begged off, sending a doctor's note to justify his inability to travel.[48] All of the witnesses were white,[49] an occurrence open to two interpretations, both equally revealing: either they were selected deliberately to influence the judicial process, or they were the people that Fleet Walker considered to be his worthiest friends.

Reasoning that all losses on his line were now properly chargeable to his "depredations," the government charged Walker with three different counts of unlawfully, knowingly, and willfully secreting, embezzling, and destroying mail involving not one but nine different packages and letters between April and the time of his arrest. On 8 December Walker entered an interim plea of not guilty. Indictments were returned nonetheless, and a trial was scheduled for 12 December, to be heard in the Eastern Division of Ohio's Southern District Court of the United States, in Columbus.

Walker's testimony speculated that the tearing of envelopes passing through his hands was due to rough handling. He denied any knowledge whatsoever of three of the envelopes presented in evidence. The government lined up at least five postal employees, including Holmes, Owen, and Montgomery, and a few of the citizens whose letters had been purloined, to counter Walker's contentions. The testimony of Deputy Marshall W. F. Harness added to Walker's problems. Harness told the court that Walker, thinking the deputy had worked up the decoy, had threatened to get even with him. When he learned that it had been Holmes responsible for the arrest, Walker, according to Harness, made "very grave threats" against Holmes.[50] The prosecution case must have left the heavier impression of truth. The jury returned a guilty verdict. The minimum sentence was a five-hundred-dollar fine or six months in jail. The judge sentenced Fleet Walker to one year in jail plus costs of prosecution. On 14 December, a U.S. Marshal delivered Walker to the Miami County prison in Troy, Ohio, an exile far across the state from his Steubenville home.[51]

This time the press carried no detailed reports of the trial. No reports of his loving wife, Ednah, clutching his hand, or his three children by his side. No reports of insults exchanged by assailant and victim. Under the headline "Sentenced" the *Steubenville Herald-Star* simply gave the verdict and its consequence, but also added that both were received "with surprise and regret by Mr. Walker's friends in this city, as they expected a verdict of acquittal."[52]

Walker himself expected acquittal. He would not accept this verdict. At some point between December and February he received a transfer from the Miami County Jail back to Jefferson County's prison, in Steubenville. At that time, the only federal penitentiary was in Leavenworth, Kansas. Federal prisoners needed a sentence exceeding one year to earn a stay there. All other inmates were contracted to various municipal and county facilities. Still, Walker was a federal prisoner, and the only possible relief from incarceration was through a presidential pardon. On 16 February 1899, Walker filed a plea with the Department of Justice requesting William McKinley's pardon. It never reached the president's desk. In little more than two weeks, an adverse ruling was on its way back to Walker, both the U.S. Attorney and the trial judge having reviewed the request negatively.[53]

Remarkably, Walker made one more plea for freedom. It revealed the depths of his despair, the degree to which legal training imbues some attorneys with a regard for the judicial process as contest rather than justice, and the degree to which Moses Fleetwood Walker was still walking the fine line between arrogance and humility. In a Negro, a measure of the latter needed always to exceed any portion of the former.

Historians in the twentieth century identified several distinct character types in slaves. Chief among them were the submissive "Sambo" facade and a more assertive but still rationally deferential "Jack" personality. Some slaves had mastered the technique of delicately mixing the two. Fleet Walker, in writing to the third assistant postmaster general on 3 April 1899, demonstrated that the technique was not unique to slaves but was in fact a universal antidote used by the socially, economically, and politically weak to combat perceived tyranny.

"Hon. Sir," Walker began. "I desire most respectfully to bring to your honorable attention some methods used by P.O. Inspectors Holmes and Owen in the case of the U.S. vs. M. F. Walker." In three handwritten pages Walker went on to detail the effrontery of the postal inspectors and the depth of his misery. It was Holmes and Owen, he maintained, who had violated postal regulations. Because they had "made up" a certain letter, it was not a "genuine" registered letter, and therefore could not have been purloined as such. The two inspectors could not lawfully place a letter in a tie-sack because postal regulation forbid interference with the mails. Walker claimed that in addressing a letter to a fictitious person, Holmes and Owen had again used methods that breached the "fidelity and impartiality demanded of every employee" of the post office. Walker never once said he had not taken the missing letter. Sadly, despite the outcome of the trial in Syracuse, he had come at this point in his life to believe that civil rights were always a casualty of the judicial process. The final paragraph was a fitting epitaph to the lowest moment in his life:

> I am a poor man, and with a family or I should attempt by every legal method to right the infamous wrong done me, an innocent man. Hoping that through my deep interest I have not exceeded moderation, I beg to remain your most humble servant
>
> Moses F. Walker[54]

If the thefts began three years before the conviction, then it was shortly after Arabella's death that Walker's despair grew deepest and, of course, his actions most desperate. When the court delivered the "body of the within named Moses F. Walker" to the Miami County jailor on 14 December 1898 – a Wednesday – the prisoner's life carried more than the grief of a spouse's death, however. As Walker succumbed to a swirl of forces that he struggled to control, the decade became a capstone on a life of thwarted potential.

The tall, lithe, handsome, intelligent charmer who had left Oberlin to become a professional ballplayer had become, in the misspent 1890s, an indigent mail robber. Walker's life had become the refuge for three forms of anger. Turned outward, the rage had assumed the shape of knives and guns and exploding artillery shells. Turned inward, it had become the soul's dark companion on which alcohol preys. Now, finally, Walker would harbor the worst of them all – anger turned to rank bitterness. It is the final anger and the most destructive. It is fed by self-deception – the bigger the lies, the deeper the bitterness.

What lies had Fleet Walker been telling himself? Obviously, many. That he could ignore the Syracuse jury's heartfelt advice to abandon alcohol, for one. (His life never lost touch with liquor. How many registered letters containing two dollars may have gone to support this relationship?) That merit could serve as a man's primary credentials. (The International Association's color line should have dissuaded him from telling himself this one.) That charm and knowledge were reliable backups when merit failed. (Unless you stole registered U.S. mail, of course.) The biggest lie was that it was possible to live with a divided heart in a divided nation.

When the Supreme Court's 1896 *Plessy v. Ferguson* decision declared that Americans would henceforth be legally separate but equal races, the ensuing wave of Jim Crow laws that defined social barriers soothed some of the white hysteria that had triggered large numbers of lynchings a few years earlier. The laws also made it clear that no one would be permitted to live in the middle of the race question. But that is the only place where Fleet Walker, first by birth and then by breeding and circumstance, was equipped to live. Being a mulatto became an even greater chore.

Accompanying the American drive to bisect the population into blacks and whites only was an ever-increasing need to belittle mulattos as the derelict, ungodly product of race mixing. The question of mulatto breeding reasserted itself. In 1893 the *Journal of the American Medical Association* published an article titled, "The Morbid Proclivities and Retrogressive Tendencies in the Offspring of Mulattoes." That same year an Ohio physician claimed that the prosperity, refinement, and physical vigor which had marked his town's mulatto population in antebellum days had virtually disappeared in the remaining families. The survivors were, he claimed, "inferior in vitality, intelligence, and consequent morality," with increased tendencies toward complete sterility.[55] Amazingly, Walker's immediate family seemed to again confirm the worst of white stereotypes for mulattos. George Price and Ednah Mason had had no children. Fleet and Ednah had no children. Of the three born to Bella and him, only Thomas had a child, a son who died in infancy of a stomach ailment.

Walker's self-hatred and his own antagonism toward mulattos would take nearly another full decade to find public expression, but the clues to their presence in 1898 laced the letter that he had sent to the post office pleading for leniency. It seemed, according to Walker, that damning pieces of evidence that he believed would have been barred by the skills of a competent lawyer, had drawn no objection from his court-appointed attorney. Poverty had, he claimed, prevented him from securing the counsel he wanted. This deficient court-appointed attorney, Walker claimed, was incapable of being shown "that unfair methods were being used." The assertions directly contradicted newspaper accounts that claimed Walker's attorney had, in fact, made a "strong fight for his client," including a motion "to throw out a part of the evidence on the ground that one of the letters was a decoy."[56] Who was this attorney, then, that Walker thought had left him so poorly defended? He was Wilbur F. King, a thirty-three-year-old mulatto.[57]

At about the same time that Arabella Walker died, three primary images of the mulatto began to emerge in African-American fiction. The first was of the tragic mulatto, intended to evoke sympathy. Surely Fleet Walker at century's end was tragic though the robbery conviction undermined his claims to sympathy. A second was that of a complex individual, sensitive to his no-win situation between two races. This figure was more likely to opt for "passing" into the white world. Indeed, between 1880 and 1925 many mulattos chose to pass for white, often relocating to hide forever the secret of their black blood. Fleet Walker was too dark, too angry, and too courageous to do the same, and thus he set out on a course that would make him most like the third type, a stout-hearted man of middle-class virtue who takes up a role as a leader of the Negro race.[58] A perfect calling in which to allow his bitterness to speak for a cause that might somehow rid him of it.

It seems unlikely that a man languishing in prison would be fit for this type of leadership, but the ambition of Fleet Walker impelled him to find an outlet for it. Baseball had once provided a stage, but the game was now many years beyond his reach, both physically and socially. The official baseball guides of the day treated the history of the Walker brothers as if it had taken place in the uncertain haze of antiquity. "Not in the recollection of the men that have been playing since 1880," reported Reach's 1896 guide, "have there been any colored players on any of the League teams. Only two colored men were played in the American Association, and that was during the infancy of that organization."[59] As if to underscore the distance, a poem appeared in the *Sporting Life* in 1898, a tribute to a former enemy, Cap Anson, who was now, like Fleet Walker, being forced to make concessions to time:

> Passing now is old man Anson,
> Base ball Gladstone of this country,
> Mighty wielder of the willow,
> Premier Pilot of young players,
> Passing now is he forever,
> Out beyond the grassy diamond
> To a life of sad seclusion.[60]

Though it may have seemed that both faced sad seclusion, Walker's education and anger equipped him for further battles in a way that Anson's singular talents could not. As calendar pages flipped toward a new century, there were no pleasant surprises awaiting the Negro population of America. But Moses Fleetwood Walker, fresh from jail, was reworking an old idea for Negro salvation, turning it into something he thought to be uniquely his, and using it to build a new stage for his talents. To do so, he would first have to become the unlikeliest of things. Fleet Walker would become a race theorist.

5

. . . .

No one could entertain higher

regard for the American white man

and his magnificent civilization than

the writer.

    M. F. Walker, *Our Home Colony*

CHAMADE

In the decade following his imprisonment for mail robbery, Moses Fleetwood Walker became a race theorist. Like all the others, he would dig a canal, clearing from his path unwanted ground and throwing it to the side. As might be expected, Walker's ambition demanded that his canal be longer than any other. While white supremacists dug theirs only through the short distance that separated bigotry from legalized segregation, Fleet Walker intended to dig his all the way to Africa. In doing so he would also create a book, a record that reflected not only the chaotic mix of beliefs that tore at his soul, but one that also asserted color as the crucial and defining ingredient in the mix.

For at least twenty years Fleet Walker and brother Weldy had thought about race relations and involved themselves in attempts to improve them. They had brought suit against segregated institutions, attempted to physically integrate others, and tried the political avenue (in 1897 Weldy had joined the efforts of Ohio blacks to be placed on state ballots through formation of the Negro Protective Party, a short-lived, Democrat-backed experiment).[1] It is unlikely, however, that at the turn of the century the Walker brothers thought of themselves as radicals. Radicalization requires transformation of emotional alienation into conscious intellectual process, and the Walkers would not fully arrive there until 1908, after wading through ever deeper currents of emotional despair.

By 1900 any hopes that some Americans held for racial harmony were slipping irretrievably away. The impermeability and permanence of baseball's color line symbolized the acceptance of caste as clearly as any Jim Crow law. As early as 1891, when President Benjamin Harrison watched a game between a colored club and a white one, the mold had been cast.[2] When the retired Cap Anson published his autobiography in 1900, he referred with impunity and without fear of public rebuke to Clarence Duval, the White Stocking mascot of the 1880s, as a "little coon," a "little darky," and a "no account nigger."[3] The game's faith in segregation was such that the Richmond correspondent for *The Sporting News* reported in 1899, "Of course, the negroes do a good share towards supporting the game. But that is no reason why they should be allowed to take part in the game against white men."[4] The absence of any sense of irony in such declarations harkened back to the patronizing rhetoric slaveholders had once embraced. Indeed, white America had in the course of several decades exchanged the physical chains of slavery for the more efficient and more ethically tolerable ones of rational separation.

Oddly enough, after 1900 science tended gradually toward a concept of culture that stressed social rather than biological determinism. By 1910 most social scientists discarded the idea that race mixture resulted in physical degeneracy, but deeply ingrained beliefs that had settled into the American consciousness during the preceding decades continued to taint academic assessments of race, and the work of propagandists in the popular press made it appear that scientific theory continued to support notions of permanent Negro inferiority.[5] The level of venom in white assertions varied according to perceived tensions, and often these continued to stem from threats of black sexuality. In 1903 U.S. Senator Benjamin Tillman cited the alleged rise in Negro rapes of white women as evidence of a black attempt to mix the races. In 1905 William Benjamin Smith's *The Color Line: A Brief in Behalf of the Unborn* declared that lower-class whites would be swamped if the tide of race mixing continued to rise. In 1907 Robert W. Schufeldt, an army physician, was more direct in giving voice to white fears. His book, *The Negro: A Menace to American Civilization,* claimed that desire drove black men "to carnally possess white maidens and women." In Negroes, he wrote, all passions and ambitions were "subservient to the sensual instinct," and this included black women as well as men.[6] The claims of Tillman, Smith, and Schufeldt were not new, however. They were merely echoing and reinforcing pronouncements that had already passed into the realm of accepted truth among whites most sympathetic to their message. The reality of collapsed relations between the races rang out in a popular turn-of-the-century minstrel song, "All Coons Look Alike to Me," which gave a melodic, lighthearted voice to the one-drop rule.

In 1900 the United States Census abandoned its classification of the Walker family as mulatto. With the exception of their forty-five-year-old servant from Ireland, Sarah Richmond, all of Fleet's household members rated the designation of *b* for black.[7] But if segregation was a relatively uncomplicated matter for many whites, if they conveniently believed that all blacks really appeared indistinguishable from one another, it was not so in the nation's black communities. The permanence, dominance, and apparent invincibility of white belief in white supremacy deeply stirred and agitated the black population. At the lowest economic levels, the only possible answer was resignation. But among those not yet economically or spiritually broken, there were two fundamental choices for responding to what had become known as simply the race question. One could continue to keep faith in eventual assimilation – social as well as economic – and thus continue to lend faith and support to white institutions and white life-styles, or one could accept the idea of racial differences and begin to seek identity in black racial pride. Both choices contained the seeds of torturous paradox, particularly for mulattos.

For the many mulattos who constituted a sizable segment of the Negro aristocracy, assimilation had already failed. Good character and good behavior had not brought acceptance or even recognition. Their aspirations for equality were diluted and lost amid the futility and ineptitude of the dark, undifferentiated masses. In fact, the existence of a multitiered structure within black society, based at least in part on lightness of skin, drew not only white derision but also the animosity of darker-skinned blacks who were similarly unaccepting of a separate and higher black class. The possibility of assimilation, then, became a matter of individual resolve, and for those who elected to continue its pursuit, it sometimes became desirable to not just act white but literally to become more white, to no longer look like "all coons."

For several decades, some blacks had made cosmetic attempts to mute their African features. The Toledo team photo of 1883 shows that Fleet Walker had by that time exchanged the soft wave of his Oberlin days for hair more severely straightened. By 1888 his photo image revealed further change. Lighting, angles, and the nuances of camera technology can play fearsome tricks on the eye – indeed, the 1889 team photo restores Walker's look to one nearly identical to that of 1883 – but the 1888 photo makes Walker appear nearly indistinguishable from his white teammates. The processed hair appears atop a face that seems lighter and more sharp-featured. If Walker was not actually altering his appearance, there were others who were. As a class the Negro elite paid homage to white standards. Late in the nineteenth century, colored newspapers stressed a subtle desire to be like whites, often emphasizing the wealth and power of the Negro elites and their indulgence in white avocations like horse breeding and training. But in the years surrounding the turn of the century, as race relations hit bottom, a rash of products attempted to exploit Negro shame with ads that promised change so startling they could scarcely be classified as cosmetic. They promised to turn blacks into whites.

"Colored people. Your salvation is at hand. The Negro need no longer be different in color from the white man." This enticement came in 1903 from Chillicothe, Ohio's, "Black-No-More." While "Black-No-More" offered sensational rhetoric, its claims were representative of all skin-bleaching lotions that combined appeals to science with rejection of deep or permanent racial differences. Between 1897 and 1905 a variety of skin whiteners – from "Imperial Whitener" to "Marwin" to "Dr. Read's Magic Flesh Bleach" – joined Black-No-More and the usual hair straight-eners in attempts to persuade Negroes that their skin structure and blood composition were identical to those of whites and that only ages of living under the tropical sun had turned their originally pale skin to black. Some of the new lotions claimed to be the breakthrough results of many years of research on pigmentation and cell structure. All assured user safety, convenience, speedy and permanent change, and some hinted that large files of testimonials supported their abilities to turn Negroes into whites.[8]

Skin bleaches that advertised regularly in black newspapers like the *Indianapolis Freeman* and the *Richmond Planet,* and in black periodicals like *Alexander's Magazine* and the *Colored American Magazine,* found a thriving market,[9] but their ineffectiveness drew many complaints. In 1905 a fraud investigation launched by the U.S. Post Office led to the revelation of the ingredients found in these miracle discoveries that could turn "mulattos perfectly white."[10] Chemical analysis showed that along with harmless substances like water, glycerin, and tincture of benzoin, the bleaches relied on mercuric chloride, a corrosive that destroyed the skin's outer layer. The investigation concluded that the bleaches had no permanent beneficial effect and could actually be injurious.[11] Nonetheless, ads con-tinued for years after the fraud charges, new charlatans arose, risking exposure for the chance at fast profits from the sale of miracle products guaranteed to "do more to advance colored people socially and commercially than showy garments or gew-gaw jewelry."[12]

The most insidious aspect of the skin bleaching ads was found in Marwin's assurance that their "wonderful discovery" would arrive "securely sealed from observation."[13] That is, purchasers attempting to flee their blackness would be spared public revelation of their betrayal. This was an important consideration, for if interest in cosmetic racial transformation was flourishing, so was the developing instinct for black nationalism, the second response to the race question.

Black nationalism, the support of "black self-sufficiency, group self-consciousness, and spiritual allegiance to Africa,"[14] became noticeable in America beginning in the midnineteenth century. Until race relations reached a new low at the turn of the century, however, the basic optimism of black Americans in eventual equality delayed its impact. As strains of white nationalism became pronounced in America and Europe, black nationalism became linked to Pan-Africanism, a belief that the fatherland had endowed all blacks around the world with a common color and cultural heritage. Oddly enough, while black nationalism was a reaction to white oppression, it leaned on the same principles and practical models as white chauvinism. For example, the claim that African heritage contributed to one's cultural traits echoed the claims of some whites that they were genetically superior in part because of their Anglo-Saxon heritage. And in many ways black nationalism reinforced white wishes for racial separation.

Accepting Africa as their spiritual homeland tied blacks in unflattering ways to the white stereotypes of a dark and primitive cultural history. The "Little Africas" that dotted American cities were derogatory white labels for slum areas. The 1904 World's Fair, in St. Louis, in the interest of the emerging science of anthropology, had brought "primitive" peoples from around the globe to St. Louis where they lived in reconstructed habitats for the edification of white American fair visitors. Some of the primitives had been forced to take part in "Anthropology Day" athletic events strewn amid Olympic events that were themselves scattered erratically amid the World's Fair program. The result was desultory spectacles in which natives attempted alien skills. Aged sprinters and unskilled "savage" shot-putters appeared as athletic incompetents. A second phase showcased what organizers deemed native skills. Among the abominations was a mud fight staged by African pygmies.

This reduction of African human life to lower animal life reached its fullest expression when, in 1906, Ota Benga, one of the World's Fair pygmies, briefly went on display in New York City's zoo. Eventually unable to adjust to the stress of life away from Africa, Benga committed suicide in 1916.[15]

The stress of being an American black and remembrance of the collective humiliation and individual hardship that color imposed presented a dilemma. Could one resist white America, embrace black nationalism, and ever hope to gain equality in the United States? It was a question no blacks, not even leaders like Booker T. Washington and W. E. B. Du Bois could answer. While the two held opposing thoughts on the means, both believed that the end of Negro aspirations should be assimilation. Their appeal to the Negro masses, however, was as *black* leaders, and their identification as such lent further weight to the idea of a separate black experience. Du Bois himself hinted at acceptance of such when he asked, "Am I an American or a Negro? Can I be both?"[16] In asking, he had accepted the basic premise that to be American was to be white. In doing so, he shed light on phenomena like skin bleaching and on a third Negro response that rejected assimilation, but also went beyond nationalism, beyond spiritual allegiance, beyond the grasp of white men. It was the response that Moses Fleetwood Walker, as race theorist, would pursue.

When he left jail at the turn of the century, Fleet Walker returned to a business he had tried briefly fifteen years earlier in Cleveland. He moved from the High Street house he had lived in while a railway clerk, and took up residence in his new place of business, Steubenville's Union Hotel at 105–7 Market Street. Ednah and the three children, all school-age, made the move with Fleet. The hotel was across the street from brother William's former saloon, though William and Maud had left town. Located at the most vital intersection in Steubenville's downtown, the hotel was to remain in the hands of the Walker family until 1939, though it would serve as more than a hotel and its proprietorship would reveal some quirks of relationship and circumstance.

In 1902 the Steubenville city directory listed Fleet as the hotel proprietor and, in the familiar pattern of lead and follow, Weldy as the hotel's clerk. The 1904–5 directory, however, designated Weldy as proprietor and Fleet and Ednah as residents. It may be that Weldy took over operations when Fleet became in those years the manager of an opera house in nearby Cadiz. It is curious, however, that inasmuch as Fleet ran the Cadiz theater on a regular basis for the next fifteen years, he was nonetheless in 1906 listed again as the Union Hotel's proprietor, while Weldy took up the role of resident.[17]

For at least a brief span of time in 1902, both brothers were more than hoteliers. In a venture in race separatism that would take its ultimate form in 1908, Fleet and Weldy Walker became the editors of a black issues-oriented newspaper, *The Equator.* Though not a single copy has survived as evidence, both brothers listed the publication in surveys they returned to Oberlin College years later. The city directory listed the paper's address as 107 Market Street and its editor as Fleet Walker. However short-lived, its ambitions must have been large. On his survey, Weldy proclaimed himself to have been just the local editor, and M. F. Walker, the editor.[18] The paper's title was a certain sign that the Walkers were flirting with the third Negro response, the one that answered Du Bois's query as to what Negroes were.

If Negroes were not Americans, why live in America? If they were African, why not live in Africa? Pair spiritual allegiance with physical presence. It was a simple solution, one that many whites – from the thoughtful to the bigoted, from Jefferson to Lincoln – had embraced for more than a century. It was important enough to draw the attention of most black leaders from David Walker to Frederick Douglass to Du Bois and Washington. It was made complex by logistics but more so by its paradox. To return to Africa meant a chance to begin anew with a society in which equality applied to blacks. It also meant an acceptance of white racial doctrine and an acceptance of a solution agreeable to many whites. It was thus perfect for a divided heart, capable of spreading the blame across two races, casting the disappointment over two continents.

If the Walkers were toying with the notion of an African return as editors of *The Equator,* they laid the possibilities aside until 1908. By then Fleet was no longer in Steubenville and Weldy was briefly removed from the Union Hotel. But in that year a new blast of anger came from Steubenville and the Walkers in the form of *Our Home Colony: The Past, Present, and Future of the Negro Race in America,* a forty-eight-page book/treatise in which its author, M. F. Walker, advocated African emigration for all black Americans. Why the six-year hiatus? As with Moses' solitary life in the immense desert, sometimes a period of quietude precedes a flourish. Maybe the thoughts begun with *The Equator* were just too compelling to leave behind; maybe they had been amplified and vivified in the years between – by the charade of primitive Africans being forced by World's Fair organizers to compete in Anthropology Day athletic events alien to their cultures, by a pygmy in a zoo, by the racial invective stirred in 1908 by the first black heavyweight titleholder, Jack Johnson. Perhaps Fleet shared the thesis of victimology later popularized by Malcolm X, who believed that black prisoners put behind bars by the white man became most accepting of a view of the white man as devil. And perhaps, while Walker's talents and some of his desires challenged him to participate in the white world, his very name issued a more persistent challenge to perform mighty deeds on behalf of the disadvantaged.

Whether there was a straw that broke the back, *Our Home Colony* was a storehouse of race theory, a lifetime's accumulated discontent unleashed. Taken as a whole, it is readable, coherent, articulate, organized. Couched in near academic language, its overall impression is of a studied and reasonable reaction to white oppression ("our own personal experience, in no way, has been allowed to bias our judgment," the preface trumpets). Deconstructed, it is the agonized outline of an autobiography, a prima facie case for a bitterly divided heart.

Our Home Colony is certainly the most learned book a professional athlete ever wrote. While the contradictions are startling and amazing, one no longer needed to wonder about the impact of white supremacists like Thomas Dixon, of black leaders like Du Bois, of the rising surety of science, the classical training of Oberlin. Fleet Walker had absorbed some of them and examined them all. "Pioneer Days," a column on Negro life in Jefferson County that appeared in the *Steubenville Herald,* regarded *Our Home Colony* as "a racial book full of hatred" written by a jealous Fleet Walker in response to another black resident's humorous autobiography.[19] It is true – there is hatred there, though its target is ambiguous. It is more exact to say it was a racial book full of emotion. Radicalization may be an intellectual process, but whatever cover dispassionate language provided to Fleet Walker, the emotional energy that launched it lingered. Maybe, as some have thought, radical resolve always comes of anger; but guilt, at copping out morally, remains a suspect as well. In that sense *Our Home Colony* is a moral offering in the guise of an ideological issue. It is understandable, then, that the most emotionally explosive portion of the book – Walker's solution of an African return – is given the most emotionally tranquil treatment.

The return of blacks to Africa through colonization – a white solution with a long tradition – or through emigration – a black nationalist answer – were two sides of the same coin. By the time of *Our Home Colony* neither movement had succeeded in resettling enough American black volunteer emigrants in Africa to ease, much less erase, tensions in the United States. Further, neither had produced any return plans that had been conceived and implemented throughout by Negroes. They had, in fact, at times ironically united white segregationists and black radicals.[20] Fleet Walker's plan, then, was unique for several reasons. First, the emigration was to be run by him and Weldy; Fleet would be the Black Moses. Second, it anticipated the unmasked anger of blacks that would make Marcus Garvey's plea for African emigration popular a decade later. Garvey, who came to the United States from Jamaica in 1916 to lead the Universal Negro Improvement Association, was hostile to white cooperative spirit in the African venture. For real, total, unambiguous separation from and rejection of whites, however, he could not top Fleet Walker, who wrote, "Even forced Emigration would be better for all than the continued present relations of the races."[21] He would defy Washington, Du Bois, and the other assimilationists. He would remove, if necessary, the previously voluntary aspect by driving the Negroes back to Africa for their own good.

Walker inserted his plea for the "entire seperation [*sic*] by Emigration of the Negro from America" two-thirds of the way into *Our Home Colony.* Historically the idea is more difficult to place. It occurred in a trough between the end of a twenty-year period (1890–1910) in which blacks demonstrated an intense interest in emigration but little concrete organization, and the more concerted and well-known efforts of Garvey. It also occurred at a time when Negroes, having shed the indistinct longing of slaves that implored Moses to work a miracle – to "Come along, Moses, don't get lost"[22] – sought instead real black leaders. There is no doubt that Walker thought of his plan and ideas as significant. Though he admitted that they were not all original, he did consider them to be opposed to those of all the leading Negro teachers and writers at work on the race problem.[23] Exactly where did Walker fit? As had been the case with his baseball career, Walker's radicalism – though its roots were sunk in the past and though it was not then readily apparent – anticipated a future moment that could not be willed into an earlier arrival.

Nearly from the time that some white Americans began transporting blacks from Africa for slavery, other whites were thinking of the possibilities for sending them back. The American Colonization Society, founded in 1817, established the colony of Liberia on the strength of funds from white philanthropists and the federal and some state governments. Before the Civil War the society transported thirteen thousand blacks to Liberia,[24] and after the war all manner of fate for the thousands of unloosed slaves was discussed, including a proposed "Colony of Linconia," in Panama.[25] But Linconia never panned out, and by the late nineteenth century the trade with Liberia consisted more of monkeys, parrots, and coffee than of colonists.[26] Between 1892 and 1900, the ACS managed to send only twenty-three colonists to Liberia. By then it seemed clear that if an African return was to take place, it would have to gain a greater share of incentive from blacks.

American blacks were ambivalent, however. In 1830, when blacks first began to convene annually to call attention to their demands, they disparaged the idea of colonization.[27] Even David Walker, a Boston black whose ideas of racial equality through violent means would have been well known to a student of Negro history like Fleet Walker (Fleet, in fact, shared this earlier Walker's characterization of American Negroes as a separate colony in bondage) was an early opponent of emigrationism. As a black intelligentsia developed in midcentury, however, and white sentiment for removal and expulsion gained momentum, Negro spokesmen reexamined emigration – and disagreed about it. In the early 1850s the National Emigration Convention of Colored Men, meeting in Cleveland, appointed agents to explore the possibilities for mass emigration to Haiti, Central America, and the Niger Valley.[28] But the famed leader Frederick Douglass adamantly resisted escapism. "No one idea has given rise to more oppression and persecution toward the colored people of this country than that which makes Africa, not America, their home," he stated.[29] Alexander Crummell, who would later spend twenty years in West Africa, believed that repudiation of the so-called Dark Continent caused blacks to take "shame at their origin and shrink from the terms which indicate it."[30]

During Reconstruction, Africa remained a conflicted homeland. Black Americans were often as intent on raising cultural standards for Africans as they were on resettling there. As the Negro institution with the greatest wealth and most viable talent, the church, particularly the African Methodist Episcopal, exerted the strongest American presence in Africa, missionaries being particularly vigorous in Liberia.[31]

During the late nineteenth century and into the early years of the twentieth, however, Bishop Henry M. Turner, of Baltimore, took advantage of the declining economic and emotional state of blacks to steer their resurgent nationalist inclinations toward renewed thoughts of Africa. Though the vast majority of educated Negroes opposed emigration, and though many attacked Turner in scathing terms, he nonetheless made inroads with the lower classes, filling them with mixed hopes of an economic and spiritual utopia. His rhetoric was itself scathing: "A man who loves a country that hates him is a human dog and not a man," he wrote.[32] To Turner, American blacks had nothing to teach the Africans. Reversing the accepted wisdom that held that exposure to America had boosted the cultural refinement of blacks, he argued instead that the race had undergone a sort of devolution in America. During a visit to Liberia he wrote that

> we poor American Negroes were the tail-end of the African races. We were slaves over here, and had been for a thousand years or more before we were sold to America. Those who think the receding

forehead, the flat nose, the proboscidated mouth, and the big flat-bottom foot are natural to the African are mistaken. There are heads here by the millions, as vertical or perpendicular as any white man's head God ever made . . . I have seen specimens of nineteen tribes, and I have not seen over 100 of them constructed on as low scale as I have seen in America.[33]

It was language meant to raise hopes, but its echoes of anthropometrically defined differences sounded perilously like that of white race theorists of the day like Edwin Cope. Cope urged in 1890 that America's surplus treasury and its navy be employed in the wholesale shipping of blacks to Africa. The facts of the case as he saw them were that American blacks were lacking in rationality and morality as determined by their organic constitution.[34]

Private entrepreneurs launched emigration ventures based on Turner's confidence that blacks would pay to return to Africa. But they cared little for the philosophy of Turner or Cope. They wished to make African emigration the font of their own prosperity. In 1894 four Birmingham whites organized the International Migration Society, seeking to charge blacks for passage to the fatherland. The IMS was just one of many small emigration companies that sought in the years up to 1910 to make a profit from the despair of American Negroes. Fleet Walker's *Our Home Colony* appeared just as the last report from Liberia – a negative one – was printed in *Alexander's Magazine* in connection with the journal's ambitious plan to take six hundred people back to Liberia.[35]

Is it possible that Fleet and Weldy Walker were among the entrepreneurs seeking economic gain from the race question? Was this the reason for advocating a forced return? Their motivation and odds are slippery. What were the chances that a onetime law student and a onetime homeopathic medical student – now an exconvict and a bartender – could lead American Negroes to a promised land? When Weldy returned an alumni questionnaire to Oberlin on 15 July 1908, he listed his occupation as "General Agent for 'Our Home Colony' and Liberian emigration," with an address at 142 Lake Erie Avenue, in Steubenville.[36] It is impossible to know if emigration was a pipedream or a concrete venture for Fleet. For ten months of the period surrounding publication of *Our Home Colony* he had stopped operations of his Cadiz theater and resided with Ednah in Gallipolis, Ohio, far south of Cadiz and Steubenville. He had been willing to lecture in connection with the book. Ultimately, however, not a single passenger sailed for Liberia under the auspices of the Walker brothers.[37]

When one is troubled by opposing feelings, ambiguity may conceal the secrets of the unconscious. When the ambiguity is announced in loud, angry tones, as with Fleet Walker, it may not look like ambiguity at all. But the African return may have signified an attempt to reject what he really desired most: intimacy with white civilization. In fact, Africa skirted in and out of focus – though it addressed its economic feasibility, *Our Home Colony* lacked a single concrete detail about emigration plans. Meanwhile the rest of the book wove an intriguing tale of self-revelation that said Moses Fleetwood Walker was not ready to leave behind white civilization. On a great array of topics, Walker held forth in splendid confusion, unable to conceal the ambivalence of his divided heart.

On the most crucial issue, the notion of racial differences, *Our Home Colony* reinforced decades of white supremacist theory: "it is contrary to everything in the nature of man," Walker wrote, "and almost criminal to attempt to harmonize these two diverse peoples while living under the same government."[38] How diverse? "When the races are so differentiated in mental and physical characteristics as the Negro and Anglo-Saxon, the government that undertakes the experiment [to unite them] rests at all times on a volcano."[39]

Walker was inconsistent on how the differences came about. Most often he argued that white oppression accounted for them, an environmentalist viewpoint. During "the Dark Period," the slavery years, the Negro was "forbidden to think," and "mental darkness brooded over the people."[40] The crushing humiliation of slavery had turned Negroes timid and subservient, forming the poor Negro character: "That he would be made false, secretive, deceitful and immoral could not fail."[41] Still, at times, Walker lapsed into passages that recalled the quasi-scientific feel of polygenesis. The Negro, he said, "is not of a migratory race, and has never been found further than twenty degrees from the torrid zone unless under force."[42] Though he had scant use for Christian principles, Walker paraphrased biblical scripture that later resounded in similar beliefs girding the separatist leanings of Malcolm X and the Black Muslims: "God hath made of one blood all nations of men to dwell on all the face of the Earth, and hath determined the time before appointed, and the bounds of their habitation."[43]

While social inequality may have exaggerated differences, Walker could not shake his insistence on natural law as a formidable shaper of alien races. As he used it, natural law was an inexact concept that seemed to include the workings and interactions of society, God, and science. It produced, amazingly, a belief in natural *inequality*. "In a state properly constituted men take their station according to their natural inequalities. Power will rest in the hands of the wisest and the best," he wrote.[44]

Obviously Walker considered himself one of the wisest and best, but the flawed American caste system meant he was to be "taken not according to his natural fitness and qualification, but that blind and relentless rule which accords certain pursuits and certain privileges to origin or birth."[45] In his most disturbing invocation of natural law, Walker declared, "There must always be a dominant and subordinate race in such cases from the very nature of mankind." While the effect on the subordinate people was "destructive of energy" and blighted and withered "every elevating sentiment of the human soul,"[46] it was nonetheless inevitable. If Fleet Walker believed this, he spent a great number of pages scolding whites, then blacks, for their inability to alter what he said was unalterable.

America's whites earned respect from Fleet Walker on several matters. He thought that they represented the "highest type of Twentieth Century Civilization," and that an overpowering love of personal liberty had been advanced and perfected among them.[47] Still, whites were often afflicted with a "lust for gain and power" which led to the development of their own "vicious habits of mind and body."[48] The spirit of caste had caused otherwise reasoning whites to "perform like wild animals," lynching blacks, burning them at the stake, and driving them from their homes.[49] But if whites were the obvious target of his grievances – the cause of the Negro's "outrage and persecution" – others lay at the bottom of his more bitter thoughts and deeply felt wrongs.

Blacks were the first. In a classic description of racial self-hatred, Walker chastised black Americans: "The Negro has no ideals of his own; nor can he have. Everything that pertains to his own ethnic type he despises, and this is done in most cases unconsciously."[50] Was he aware, then, of his own contempt for black culture? The Negro, he said, had no history with respect to governments, constitutions, and laws. Though free Negroes had fought during the Civil War with "the desperation and intrepidity born of the love for liberty" (one might almost surmise that his father had served in the Colored Union troops – he did not), he found blacks to be as timid and passive as their white stereotypes proclaimed them. Without the war's assistance the Negro might still "lay asleep" in bondage. Though he thought blacks had innate powers of mind and body that might blossom if they emigrated from America, it was a strange prediction inasmuch as they would have to show their capabilities in Africa, a place Walker astoundingly found no irony in labeling "the very midst of intellectual and moral darkness."[51]

The most scathing insults – indirect ones, of course – he reserved for himself, Moses Fleetwood Walker, the mulatto product of white and

Negro sexual relations. Mulattos had always borne the brunt of society's fear and disapproval of race mixing. At various times, some Negroes had preached intermarriage as the solution to the race problem. After the turn of the century this proposition retained its repugnance among whites. It lost favor as well among blacks, for whom segregation and black nationalism were producing an exaggerated animosity against interracial unions. There was, in particular, an intense hatred among the mulatto elite of mixing between white men and Negro women, an association that recalled the "pernicious pattern" of slavery.[52] Walker combined this dislike of mulattos with early white race theory to arrive at a denunciation – nearly renunciation – of his very existence: "Even were miscegenation desirable the laws of Nature seem to oppose it. It is impossible to make a hybrid race of men. The law of reversion to the original stock prevails as well among men as among the lower animals."[53] The one-drop rule had overwhelmed self-knowledge and caused even the likes of Fleet Walker to misbrand themselves, to accept the characterization of themselves as human mules. Though he was a hybrid, he denies such a creature could exist. He was now a "son of Africa," and the guilt and hatred he felt from the presence of white blood in his veins oozed out.[54] It spread in a way that added weight to the possibility that he was part of the pernicious pattern, that at least one of his grandfathers had been white, at least one of his grandmothers black.

Walker scorned the idea of interracial sex, calling it a "crime that will ultimately sap all good from the American home."[55] He held black women accountable for it. In this, he shared the belief of Edgar G. Murphy and others of the time. In 1904 Murphy wrote the *Problems of the Present South,* which maintained that race mixing resulted from white men uniting with lower-class Negro women "who had not had a chance to develop middle-class standards of sexual purity."[56] While Walker shifted initial blame to white masters, who made the Negro cabin a "harem," and though he regarded the "concubinal white man" as "a lecherous being," he held an even lower opinion of Negro women who bedded down with whites.[57] He rarely lapsed into a forgiving tone when discussing them. He thought it marvelous that "there are so many virtuous and moral Negro women," and recognized that the "Negro woman is not by nature more immoral than the white woman," merely more vulnerable to an acquired desire for the "alien" ideal of an Anglo-Saxon partner. But this recognition took a nasty turn when he pinpointed the cause for the inability of Negro women to resist the temptations of an immoral life: "The struggle for existence and a disposition to ape [an interestingly Freudian choice of words] after the ideals of the dominant race are too much for her feeble intellect and will."[58]

Maybe this all revolved around sex. "Hundreds of Negro women," he mourned a bit enviously, "do for white men what they refuse to do for men of their own race." This made the Negro concubine "a human without the least trace of moral sense."[59] In a passage that presaged the association of mulattos in the 1920s with the salacious activities of nightlife in Harlem, Chicago, and other cities, Walker noted that Negro concubines seemed to be "honored rather than ostracised."[60] In language that mirrored the sentiment of white racists who believed black females were predisposed to carnal passion, Walker said that the Negro girl could be taught art, music, and literature, "but without morals, she will become a concubine at the first opportunity!"[61] Further, he thought that American Negro women could never "develop that high and pure morality which is the bulwark and pride of every civilized people."[62] A Victorian notion, certainly.

As if the carelessly spread charge of concubinage was not enough, Walker went on to berate Negro women on one more point. He ridiculed their acceptance of white beauty standards. This matter of appearance was a sore point among mulattos, who often chose unevenly from Negro and Caucasian beauty standards in quest of an acceptable look. Madame Azalia Hackley, for example, in offering advice to Negro girls, claimed kinky hair was a mere product of Africa's torrid sun and dark skin an indicator of "rare psychic powers." Beautiful eyes, strong and attractive teeth, and fine voices distinguished Negro women. Still, she found their mouths "too large," their lips "too thick" from allowing their mouths to hang open, and their noses too broad from grinning, a habit she advised "must cease."[63] Aware of skin bleaching and personally familiar with hair straightening, Walker said it was rare to find a young black girl or boy who was not "trying to turn Anglo-Saxon." Part of the cause was Negro mothers who bought for their children "white dolls with curly hair and blue eyes."[64] His focus on appearance ideals and low morals incites curiosity as to how Ednah Jane Walker, a light-skinned product of miscegenation, a learned woman of social standing, and the owner of beautiful straight hair felt about her husband's unflattering remarks and the inescapably bleak standing black women held in his world.

The group of lowest standing in his hierarchy was not the women, however, but his own – the offspring of black and white. While he claimed that concubinal black women were proud of their light-colored children, Walker could find no cause for pride. In cruel and blistering prose he damned them all:

What is to prevent this progeny from being worse than animal? Such creatures are more dangerous to society than wild beasts; for these last can easily be hunted and shot, while the former go on procreating their lecherous kind without hindrance.[65]

Was he making a subconscious plea to be destroyed for the good of society? How dangerous did he think he was? Was removing the Negro to Africa for the good of the Negro or for the good of white America? His sense of the danger was, like all things, split. He tweaked white fears by saying that "it would surprise the whites how many of their fair daughters" Negro men would select if free to make their own choices.[66] But he also said that if whites did not soon settle the race problem through deportation, the result would be a reign of terror directed at Negroes "such as the world has never seen in a civilized country."[67]

The conflict within must have been draining and wearisome for a man now five decades old. He had no faith in any institutions. The book made mention of Booker T. Washington, W. E. B. Du Bois, and H. M. Turner, but Negro politicians, he said, "have never done the race any good."[68] One machinist, bricklayer, or carpenter was worth a dozen congressmen or judges.[69] Even workplace equality, however, could not provide social equality, and anything less than social equality promoted the "damnable and blighting caste spirit."[70] Likewise, education was a useless acquisition. No doubt recalling the personal experience of his playing days, he reminded his readers that "an educated Negro is thrown from a hotel or theatre just as certainly as an ignorant one."[71] That left only religion, the refuge and hope of his father, Moses W. Walker.

God had made inroads into Fleet's consciousness, though not enough to foster confidence in a spiritual solution. Many years later he again attended Methodist services, and in 1908 Weldy professed to "Catholic proclivities," an oddity inasmuch as the Catholics were not particularly sympathetic to the Negro plight. But the two seemed to have had no faith that God might intervene on their behalf. Fleet did hint at divine intervention when he deemed the Civil War a national calamity sent as natural punishment for the immoral course of slavery – but God was not the answer in 1908. In fact, Walker thought God had endowed people with the means to meet their own needs; if they failed to use them, they could "sit until the end of time waiting for outside help."[72] Furthermore, he did not believe that the Christian principle taught "that alien races can unite in the same state to their mutual welfare."[73]

Ambivalence about a higher being, the despair and rage he felt in America, and the hope that it could be concealed in the unemotional language of academia were summed up in the epigraph Walker selected for *Our Home Colony:* "*Ergo Agite, et, Divum Ducunte Qua Jussa, Sequamur.*" It came from Virgil's *Aeneid,* and translated it meant "Therefore, let us follow where the commands of the gods lead." Responding to the vague enticements of Virgil is a far cry from heeding the summoning chamade of African drumbeats, and for a man of modern culture those drumbeats must have sounded faint next to the symphony of white America. Moses Fleetwood Walker was of America, and his gods, unjust or not, were those of white men. Despite the proposal of *Our Home Colony,* their commands did not direct him to Africa. Like Moses, he was not destined to reach the Promised Land. Fleet may have known better than anyone that his canal could never stretch to an unseen homeland. It was dug energetically but ultimately futilely, in too many directions. Fleet Walker could not follow one narrow channel, as the white race theorists did, because at bottom he did not have their certainty. The divided heart may have kept him from Africa – when he died he had yet to apply for a passport to anywhere outside the United States – but he was not yet out of ambition.[74]

Fleet Walker had one last chapter to write, and like the others it would provide a startling mix of gumption and concession, and a continuing effort to find a livable place in what was essentially a white world. This was understandable. Though he had picked up and moved many times, Walker acknowledged that "the love of home and country is an original sentiment of the human soul."[75] For most of the next fifteen years his home was Cadiz, Ohio. It was an unlikely location for an old ballplayer's second career in public entertainment.

6

· · · · · · · · · · · · · · · · ·

The evidence is that there are depths beyond which an

intellectual process cannot go. The evidence is that there are

aspects of your own identity so strongly established that they

cannot be penetrated by conviction, not to mention thought.

There are things about our own identity that we cannot alter

by decision.

Howard Senzel, *Baseball and the Cold War*

End Credits

Cadiz is a long way from Africa, but its location southwest of Steubenville and northwest of Mount Pleasant forms a small triangle in eastern Ohio with the two childhood homes of Fleet Walker. Nearly equidistant from both, Cadiz became an appropriate way station for the divided heart, as close to and as far from trouble and buried intimacy as it dared to live. Alas when Walker settled in Cadiz, he selected a final career that would continue to aggravate his heartache and immerse him more deeply in the paradox to which his life had become addicted. Division and its consequences were things Moses Fleetwood Walker could not, after a half-century, alter by decision.

Following the adventure of publishing *The Equator,* Fleet had taken up a new calling in Cadiz in 1904, leaving operation of the Union Hotel to Weldy. Though Fleet, Ednah, and all three children remained in the Steubenville directory through 1906, only Cleodolinda, the oldest, was still listed as a student. That year Thomas, the oldest son, married Jeannette Austin, of Wheeling. Within two years, Cleodolinda also married; she left the Steubenville area and would subsequently live on each of the nation's coasts. By 1908, when *Our Home Colony* was published and Fleet and Weldy announced the Liberian emigration scheme, Fleet and Ednah had moved permanently from Steubenville.[1]

In 1908 youngest son George, Weldy, Thomas, and Jeannette left the

Union Hotel to live together at 215 South Court while Thomas tried his hand at a sales position. The hotel did not leave the care of the Walker family, however. Fleet's sister, Mary, had married again in 1897. She and her second husband, Cyrus Pryor, originally from Virginia, ran the hotel in 1908. The next year the Pryors moved to Youngstown, and Weldy, his two nephews, and Jeannette returned to the hotel. Thomas took up the proprietorship formerly held by his father, his Uncle Weldy, and his Aunt Mary. George worked at the hotel before leaving in 1921; Thomas, Jeannette, and Weldy remained at the Union Hotel for nearly two decades beyond that.[2] It seems evident from later occurrences that Fleet maintained ties with his Steubenville family, but in moving to Cadiz he was able to put a bit of distance between himself and what had turned out to be an unhappy homecoming from Syracuse, a period of time laced with loss, poverty, and, finally, jail. The new livelihood he found in Cadiz would enforce the distance for nearly the rest of his life.

Fleet and Ednah Walker began working in entertainment shortly after the turn of the century. An early reference to Walker as showman placed him in Cadiz in March 1902, showing Edison's latest stereopticon slides of the Spanish War and "singing all the latest songs." Later that month he, Ednah, and Henry Tuck toured Ohio, West Virginia, and Pennsylvania, making their first foray into moving pictures by giving kinetoscope exhibitions, chiefly at churches, "with considerable success." For some months, Fleet and Ednah gave their exhibitions, sometimes alone, sometimes together, sometimes in city halls, sometimes in churches. In late June the *Cleveland Gazette* reported that the couple had just returned from a "lecture tour" of the south.[3] Their successes must have outstripped that of Fleet and Weldy's short-lived newspaper, *The Equator,* and their visits to Cadiz must have convinced them that their talents for public entertainment and the audiences in that town were a good match.

Cadiz (pronounced CAD-is by its natives) was a picture postcard of small town America when the Walkers moved there. Merchants ringed the town's center, surrounding the Harrison County Courthouse. The business that Fleet and Ednah Walker took over in April 1904 was directly across the street from the courthouse, in a splendid red brick building referred to simply as the Opera House. The couple eventually moved into an apartment on its second floor, the better for overseeing their new daily work as the town's foremost entertainment brokers.

After fifteen years out of baseball, Walker was again an entertainer, though now the exhibitor rather than the exhibited. The Opera House hosted opera, live drama, and motion pictures. It also rented out its space for graduation ceremonies, dances, vaudeville, and minstrel shows. It was the last of these that was playing in the month that Walker took over operations from E. M. Brown. For a man still four years short of delivering the biting observations of *Our Home Colony,* this must have been a disappointing booking to accept. To earn profits, however, Walker would have to present what the public wanted to see. When the Cadiz public wanted a parody of shuffling, dancing, singing, childlike, happy Negroes, Walker obliged them. In return for his forbearance and cooperation in placing white interests first, the townspeople's patronage kept his theater open for the next decade and a half while Walker adapted to the changing demands of theater operation and his place amid the town's social order.

In choosing the entertainment business, he again courted controversial situations. Stepping into the midst of popular culture was not like running a hardware store. Even in the days before the movie industry came to regard itself as a self-conscious sculptor of popular belief, theater and film were more than spectacle; they were conducive to the "play of ideas,"[4] and thus provided stages and screens for viewing and interpreting both personal and social conflicts.

At the turn of the century, art and science – always at odds in public perception – were actually blending in theater entertainment into a medium perfect for Fleet Walker. Raised in an age of increasing faith in science, Walker had shown himself to be open to its use in constructing race theory or in the design of artillery shells. The complex machinery of filmmaking and projection, the mechanical possibilities inherent in the efficient use of a reel of celluloid, provided new ground for invention and development. At the same time the connection of motion pictures to the origins of screen practice – the magic lantern traditions of the seventeenth century[5] – connected them to art, a lure for the showman in Walker. His role in both turned out to be less than he probably would have liked.

Debate and confusion over the advance of motion picture technology was rampant in the late nineteenth century, but by 1891 inventors were well on their way to a vertical-feed motion picture camera. At that time kinetoscope parlors allowed individual viewing of kinetographs. Among the first subjects of the herky-jerky, black-and-white images were bouts of ratting, cockfighting, boxing, and wrestling, as well as posing displays of famed Austrian strongman, Eugene Sandow. The use of sports in the parlors was fitting inasmuch as Thomas Edison had reworked some of the ideas of Edouard Muybridge in developing his film technology (he later denied any participation by Muybridge).[6] Muybridge had, beginning in 1877, claimed his niche in film evolution with motion studies of horses and human athletes (it was his photographs that settled a debate as to whether all four hoofs of a running horse ever left the ground simultaneously). After 1895 inventors in four nations were simultaneously inventing projection machines that left viewers astonished at the lifelike images now thrown onto screens in front of them. The machines astonished a few operators as well, often overloading electrically and delivering painful shocks.[7] Between then and the time that Walker became an operator, the shocks had lessened and much of the flicker and jump of the pictures had been smoothed out. Still, Walker tinkered with the machinery, hitting in his later years on a technical improvement in the use of reels.

With regard to the showmanship of film, a more profound change had occurred just prior to his assumption of management. In their first decade, the presentation of motion pictures called for exhibitors to play creative roles. Motion pictures originally shared space and time with Fleet and Ednah's original entertainment fraternity: lecturers who presented travel slides, lecturers who changed voices to simulate the different characters, and exhibitors of more traditional entertainment forms, like singing and dancing. Motion pictures adapted to diverse settings. They were shown between acts of plays, in "black" tents at carnivals, in storefront theaters, and as complete evenings of entertainment in local churches or opera houses.[8] Because each of the first productions were short, one-shot films, the exhibitor was responsible for assembling the order of the program in understandable, coherent ways and sometimes for enhancing it through the use of bands, bells, whistles, and water. After 1900, however, the production companies themselves assumed greater editorial responsibility, and the exhibitor had less leeway in creative arrangement.

If his scientific or artistic talents were thus blunted in the early going, Walker was nonetheless thrust into a competitive fray that would test his business skills. In the few years before Walker became manager at the Opera House, the movie industry was making important transitions from the unrelated series of short films to single subject films to story films. The most commercially successful of these, Edison's "The Great Train Robbery," led story films in a flourishing business that spawned the nickelodeon theater.

The nickelodeon craze exploded in 1905, putting Fleet Walker's entertainment experience on the cusp of an industry revolution. Nickelodeons were specialized storefront theaters showing only motion pictures, eschewing the diversity of fare that characterized larger places like Walker's Opera House. The five-cent charge democratized moviegoing and immediately threatened burlesque, vaudeville, melodrama, and other theater programs.[9] For a brief time Walker had competed with the town's Driving Park, a track that featured a three-horse race program, with the fine local baseball team that for several seasons had the services of George Sisler, a future Hall of Famer, with the occasional trip to the big city – Pittsburgh, where the nickelodeon boom began, was just sixty-five miles east on the Panhandle Railroad – with the yearly extravaganza of the Chautauqua summer outing, and with special attractions like the World's Fair train that passed through Cadiz Junction in 1905. Now nickelodeons would force him to compete as well with other screen practitioners.

By December 1906 there were more than three hundred nickelodeons open in thirty-five states. Nearby Youngstown, Ohio, had twenty by April 1907.[10] The nickelodeons that opened in Cadiz in the five years between 1905 and 1910 are hard to track accurately. A "Nichelodeon" accompanied the county fair; the Hines Nickelodeon operated sporadically from the old post office building; there was, at least in 1909, a Wonderland Moving Picture Theatre; an Italian family, the Maffeos, ran a nickelodeon. At least once in 1910 the Cadiz newspaper even listed Walker as proprietor of the Nickelodeon. Even E. M. Brown, the same man who had turned over the reigns of the Opera House to Walker, decided to chance the nickelodeon business. As Walker's first competition, Brown, who also ran a clothing store, converted a storefront in 1906 into a beautifully appointed and brilliantly lit nickelodeon that immediately drew large crowds. As they did everywhere, the nickelodeons tested the viability of the mixed offerings of older theaters. In 1910 competition from moving pictures drove the number of shows at the Opera House to a new low. Walker countered by throwing dances with a ten-cent admission, drawing crowds as large as four hundred from Cadiz and the surrounding countryside.[11]

Walker outlasted the competition. By the end of 1912 Cadiz had just one picture show – his. Still, if nickelodeons had created a new, specialized spectator – the moviegoer – that threatened his business, why hadn't Walker turned exclusively to showing movies? Other opera houses in other towns had done so. The answer had at least in part to do with Walker's self-perceptions with regard to character and class. Just as in his playing days, when baseball's determination to rise above its tarnished image had urged its players to an off-field life-style consistent with Victorian behavioral standards, the mass appeal of entertainment in the early 1900s required him to walk a tightrope between common public taste and social elitism. For Fleet Walker, former collegian and former inmate, former ballplayer and aspiring businessman, the balancing act must have been exquisite agony.

Nickelodeons revealed the outlines of social caste. The nickel admission annihilated class distinctions that places like the Opera House made overt. Though he had matched the five-cent charge in presenting his earliest one-reel shows, Walker maintained a price hierarchy for the live entertainment that came to Cadiz. In fact, in 1908, after his ten-month hiatus in Gallipolis, he secured "motion drama talking pictures" for the Opera House, a gimmick that drew record attendance (and is not to be confused with the 1920s synchronization of film with recorded sound), interspersed the reels with vaudeville acts, and charged two rates: fifteen cents for general admission and a quarter for reserved seats.[12] This was usual procedure for the opera houses that clung to their reputations as the centers of local society. Their vaudeville shows were considered high class, and supplementing them with a few reels of film was a way to allow respectable people to see movies without resorting to the vulgar appeal of the nickelodeon.

Women, children, and the working class went to the nickelodeon. And, despite the wishes of social reformers to have movies join sports in helping to Americanize immigrants through exposure to themes of hard work, discipline, family, and sexual control, the reels in nickelodeons often lampooned authority. Nickelodeon programs changed twice weekly in 1905. By 1907 they changed almost daily and the reduced number of educational shows contrasted with those being shown in the opera houses. Though the distinct exhibition systems that served high-class theaters and nickelodeons grew closer over time,[13] they remained different enough that Walker's Opera House continued a price hierarchy for admission even in later years when he would show movies only. By and large he retained during his entire tenure the pre-1907 idea of a "show," continuing to offer a range of entertainment experiences that hinted at different levels of class and culture. A little class went well with his learned notions of society and his well-groomed appearance. For notable occasions Walker decked himself in a silk hat and a formal swallow-tailed coat.[14] But like *The Life of Moses*, a 1909 film spectacle that tried to portray the exotic look of foreign and ancient landscapes with one-dimensional painted backdrops, the entrepreneurial life of Moses F. Walker presented a picture that lacked the perspective of a fuller reality. Beneath the appearances sat great irony.

Unlike nickelodeon owners, whose backgrounds often matched those of their patrons, motion picture exhibitors in theaters were often of high social standing. They were thus vulnerable to the campaign for uplift that became increasingly strident during the Progressive Era. As popular perception drifted toward an assumption that movies aspired to reality or an illusion of the real world, social reformers demanded that the theater experience, from show content to ambience, aspire to moral rectitude. One result was that operators tried to accommodate the public demand for theaters to add restrooms, nurseries, ushers, refreshments, elaborate decor, and to drop vaudeville acts from their programs. Another was that they attempted to separate themselves from the other "recruiting stations of vice"[15] to which reformers compared them. The two most notorious were the saloon and the pool hall.

Even as darkened movie houses struggled with respectability, reformers had to admit that the "warmth and social life"[16] at the motion picture show was preferable to spending time in a saloon. Walker's Opera House did not compete, theoretically anyway, with liquor. In 1874 the Women's Crusade had first closed saloon doors in Cadiz; after a twenty-five year fight, they were shut for good.[17] By 1904 Prohibition political candidates were touting Cadiz as a model antisaloon town.[18] Liquor continued to find illegal outlets, prompting Walker in 1910 to insert into an ad for a country dance the warning: "no one admitted under the influence of alcohol."[19] Despite Fleet's past negative associations with alcohol, however, he continued to drink, and the Walker family in Steubenville continued to dispense liquor from the Union Hotel's bar.

The Union Hotel also operated a poolroom. Fleet's son George ran it for awhile. Pool halls carried an air of immorality, sharing with saloons the stigma of unproductive time, an inefficiency bearing a sinful quality in Progressive America. When a new pool hall opened in Cadiz in 1910, bringing the total to four, the mayor declared it off-limits to boys under eighteen unless accompanied by their fathers. A county citizen wrote to the *Cadiz Sentinel* to ask about the hall. "If we guess right," he wrote, "it is a loafing place, where men fool away their time and waste their money."[20] Fleet's later experience with a pool hall indicated that it was a milieu, like the saloon, that he did not find repellent. So it was that Fleet Walker lived again with paradox, unable to turn his back on either side of a clearly divided issue, seeking a reputation as an efficient purveyor of enlightening entertainment while living close to the roots of moral decay as defined by upstanding members of the middle class.

If the vices of drink and gambling and loafing could fell a man's character and undercut his pretensions to class, character was also, as always, a line of demarcation between the races. How much character could really be expected of a black man? Fleet Walker's tenure as a theater manager would again make him a public test case for answering that question. The combination of his public ambitions and his private yearnings and beliefs would yield some puzzling results.

In terms of race relations Cadiz offered nothing extraordinary in the early twentieth century, which is to say it was for all intents and purposes segregated. The eastern Ohio area, whose population of former slaves and vigorous participation in the Underground Railroad had once made it a progressive outpost of race relations (Cadiz had been a busy stop – three routes in, three out), now strained under its legacy of tolerance, which did not mesh well with the national inclination to regard separation as inevitable. The nearby community of McIntyre, the home founded by manumitted slaves, was, early in the twentieth century, adjudged by an area historian to have been a failure, undone in part by the "weird superstitions" and the fervor that marked its religious "bush meetings," and by the tendency of its residents to "Degenerate and Almost Relapse into Barbarism."[21] In Cadiz black children attended the "colored school" named for black poet Paul Dunbar. The segregation was perhaps one of the reasons Fleet Walker's children had stayed in Steubenville until 1906, completing their educations in integrated schools. There were just a few blacks of social distinction in Cadiz: the owner of a tin shop who prospered making tin roofs, the principal of the colored school, a barber who catered to the white trade, a clerk or two.[22] None were worthy of attending the town's Chautauqua, an annual summer gathering at which the prosperous whites from town pitched large tents at the fairgrounds for a week of lectures, ballgames, and picnicking. The only black faces in Chautauqua tents belonged to those who went along as maids and cooks.[23] Now, though, there was a black businessman operating public entertainment in the town's center.

In terms of cultural trends there was nothing extraordinary about the relationship of the entertainment industry to race, which is to say that for all intents and purposes blacks served as a foil for white dominance. In the first decade of film, the 1890s, it had been the misfortune of blacks that one of the first prominent exhibitors had been a former minstrel manager; hence he made films like *Shooting Craps, Who Said Watermelon?* and *Prizefight in Coontown,* popular movie shorts that perpetuated stereotypes of African Americans as childlike, unsocialized beings who carried guns and razors. After the transition to story films, production companies merely lengthened the humiliation, turning out racial comedies like *The Chicken Thief* and *A Nigger in the Woodpile.*[24] Film may have been an Americanizing agent for immigrants, but it did not offer any evidence that assimilation was a possibility for blacks. Because theater owners infrequently ran newspaper ads in the silent film era, relying instead on large, colorful posters and the distribution of handbills, the program of features that Fleet Walker ran at the Opera House in his first ten years are irrecoverable. With regard to race, however, two things are certain: Walker continued to present minstrel shows; and the Opera House was segregated on a de facto basis, the blacks sitting, as they did in many cities, in the balcony, or what the Cadiz children called Peanut Heaven.[25] Just where would Fleet Walker, a mulatto, have seated himself?

Being mulatto, of course, was not quite the same as being black. In many ways it was now worse. As race relations tended toward deeper and deeper divisions, both blacks and whites held mulattos in greater contempt. This was as true in Cadiz as anywhere else.[26] The 1908 publication of *Our Home Colony* hinted that a resentful Fleet Walker was, as the first decade came to a close, living on the fence again, clinging to a hope that the obvious signs of his merit and intelligence would eventually confer social equality upon him. *Our Home Colony* advocated race separation, and in 1910 he was still delivering related addresses on the race question.[27] Yet here he was in Cadiz running a theater in which he cooperated with white devices for impairing the social status of blacks. His own social schizophrenia was linked to his position as Opera House entrepreneur as well as his continued membership in segregated secret fraternal orders. His associations with the Knights of Pythias had continued after his move from Steubenville, and as a resident of Cadiz in 1909 he had received the commandery degree in Masonry.[28] Most revealing, however, was that, among all the white faces at the Chautauqua Park athletic events, there in 1909 was the fifty-two-year-old Fleet Walker, competing for and *winning* a three-dollar hat in the contest, "Catcher Throwing to Second Base." A measure of the tension his presence carried came the next day when only the *Cadiz Republican* reported his victory. The other town paper, the *Sentinel,* while it did not delete the contest, listed the runner-up as the winner, making no mention at all of M. F. Walker.[29]

Walker's double-edged social standing would have magnified in Cadiz the impact of a 1910 film event. The year had already brought the unsettling news that racial prejudice had "slowly but surely eaten its way into the social vitals" of Oberlin College[30] when, in July, the nation's first black heavyweight boxing champion, Jack Johnson, stirred racial hostility across the country by defeating former champ Jim Jeffries, and, much worse, consorting with white women. Now through the miracle of motion pictures Johnson was scheduled to visit towns all over America. Those who had been unable to see the fight live would be able to see Johnson play the "Great Antagonist," with Jeffries in his supporting role as the "Great White Hope." The fight had touched off riots. The film of the fight threatened to widen the arena of conflict.

Previously boxing had been an anomaly in the film industry. Along with passion plays it was a form of entertainment whose disreputable standing was somehow mediated by the screen, cinematography strangely sanitizing its image.[31] The Johnson fight reversed this. It showed why the color line in professional sport was at least as important as any Jim Crow law. Sports offered physical and damning evidence contrary to white images of the black as an inept, docile servant. Here was Jack Johnson, supreme black warrior, conqueror of white men, seducer of white women, his celluloid image magnified by the big screen a thousandfold. It was truly frightening, a cause for hysteria.

All across the country whites panicked. They implored city officials to ban the film. In Baltimore, the secretary of the city's Merchants and Manufacturers Association, presumably a fair sampling of middle-class white businessmen, wrote to the mayor:

> Our greatest fears of the arousing of the senseless, incompetent and weak race of negroes by the victory of the black man in a physical contest with a broken white, have been fully realized and the end has not yet come . . . The negro must be suppressed, and he will be. But the best citizens must do all that is possible to prevent outbreaks and everything that tends to irritate . . . The black man . . . is an inferior human being and the sooner and more completely he realizes it the better for him.[32]

Maryland, among other states, banned the film. In issuing prohibition statements, governors and mayors stressed that blacks saw Johnson's victory as racial gain because they were incapable of distinguishing between reality and meaningless sport.[33] It is obvious in retrospect that the need of whites to trivialize sport in these proclamations simply underlined the extent to which they in fact regarded it as influential and deadly serious.

So, Jack Johnson never made it to Baltimore. Did his menacing film image visit Cadiz? It is unlikely. The Cadiz papers reported the fight results, the *Republican* remarking that "many of the negroes appear to think it a triumph of their race, instead of a contest between the lowest of the races."[34] They also followed with interest the initial attempts of a Columbus promoter to secure local rights and show it there, the attempt expected to guide the rest of the state. But the matter then dropped forever out of the Cadiz press. Fleet Walker, then, may never have had to make a decision on the film, but the possibility must have raised his anxiety. To show the fight would have been to court disaster among his white patrons; to suppress it would have been to deprive the black community of its most triumphant victor in the white world. Walker, though hostage in some respects to white demands, was not immune to black interests. Later that year the Opera House presented an "Hour With Paul Dunbar," a crowded show whose proceeds went to the Dunbar School for a piano.[35] Displeased with a second-class role in the entertainment world, some blacks bought and operated theaters for black clientele. By 1913 there were an estimated 214 of these nationally.[36] The Cadiz Opera House was not one of them, and it would be another five years before film again escalated racial tension and put Walker on the hot seat. During the interim, developments in the nature of the business created new challenges for him.

Increasingly after 1910, complex projection technology, the unionization of projectionists, legal battles over cameras, the adoption of a rental system for film distribution, new licensing requirements, and behind-scenes alliances made the screening of films a chaotic process. In fact, the attempts by the powerful to make the motion picture industry a "game of freeze-out" gave an advantage to the more highly competitive exhibitors.[37] As movie palaces began to replace the smaller and shabbier nickelodeons, and the "feature film" (used to describe any multireel film after 1909) became acceptable among the middle class, blue collar crowds waned. Fleet Walker, professional competitor and manager of an elegant building, was well positioned to prosper amid the changes.

The Opera House continued to offer a full and varied entertainment slate. The theater booked magicians, stage plays, vaudeville acts, dances, school commencements, and movies. The Maffeos sold their nickelodeon in August 1912. Six months later it was out of business. By November the final competitor, the Rose Theater, also folded, leaving the Opera House as the only moving picture show in Cadiz.[38] Often it hosted shows that had already played in larger towns like Steubenville or Akron, but Cadiz was no backwater refuge for washed up performances. On a good Saturday night, films drew five hundred or more viewers. When exceptional features played, such as the 1913 "sensation of the century," Edison's "Laughing, Singing and Talking Pictures" (Edison had put together ten pictures that synchronized a phonograph recording with the lip movements of the performers), attendance went higher.[39] After 1908 large theaters employed sound systems and actors behind the screen for narration. In smaller houses, the owner, his wife, child, or a piano player was pressed into service.[40] Ednah Walker was already an Opera House employee; she took tickets and won friends among the townspeople. Whether she or Fleet also did time on piano or behind the screen is unknown, though their previous stints with stereopticon views would have prepared them for active participation. The Opera House did have a piano in the hallway atop a very steep set of stairs. The steps and the crowds helped to close the building for a short time.

Actually, public safety watchdogs in the Progressive Era were interested in more than steep steps. When the state inspector came to the Opera House in the fall of 1912, he requested an aisle be opened to the fire escape and informed the Walkers that he anticipated that a state law would soon require steel cages for film operators. Several months later, in February 1913, the Opera House closed temporarily while awaiting a new steel and asbestos cage.[41] At one other point in Walker's management the theater closed for two weeks when the town electric plant burned. Two quarantines also shut it briefly.[42]

As he moved toward his sixtieth birthday, however, rolling with the ever-changing terrain of twentieth-century entertainment, only one moment might have derailed Fleet Walker as theater operator. The demystification of screen practice had, even in the seventeenth century, relied on the waning of belief in ghosts, witch burnings, and other instruments of mystical terror.[43] In 1915 the screen's lifelike images may have awed moviegoers but they were not a concern for genuine fright. But the release that year of the finest artistic work the cinema had yet produced did indeed strike terror in the hearts of the country's blacks and the operators of motion picture theaters.

D. W. Griffith's *The Birth of a Nation,* a film version of Thomas Dixon's *The Clansman,* reworked the "lessons" of the Civil War in a twelve-reel extravaganza. It was a paean for the Ku Klux Klan and white supremacy. In many scenes there were close-ups of leering Negroes (some of them whites in blackface makeup) lusting after white women. Regardless of whether they were calculated to raise white fears and spur hostility toward blacks, that was the effect. Released by Paramount, which was also circulating at the time a film called *The Nigger,* Griffith's work brought together art, technology, advertising, and racism in a "malicious conspiracy."[44]

Dixon, working in the film's behalf, circumvented the review of the National Board of Censorship of Motion Pictures, using connections to privately show the film to and receive an endorsement from President Woodrow Wilson. Though Wilson quickly retracted his approval, the film's widespread screening created a controversy not unlike that of the Johnson-Jeffries fight, though for opposite reasons. Blacks protested the showing of *The Birth of a Nation,* occasionally breaking into segregated theaters to disrupt it, but rioting seldom.[45] Sources have disputed whether the film was banned in Ohio; in the immediacy of its first release, the Supreme Court upheld Ohio's intent to restrain it. The Cadiz newspapers never mentioned the controversy. Did Fleet Walker have to make a decision on showing Griffith's masterpiece? Again, it seems unlikely though indeterminable. The Opera House never ran an ad for it, but Walker used newspaper ads irregularly anyway. James Johnson worked as a teenager for Fleet Walker, first passing out handbills and later as a projectionist. He claims *The Birth of a Nation* and *The Last Days of Pompeii* as two of his first movie recollections at the Opera House. A contemporary of Johnson's, the daughter of the operators who eventually succeeded Walker in Cadiz, also believed the film was shown.[46] The film has achieved such cultural notoriety over the years that it is difficult positively to attribute their familiarity with the epic to a showing at the Opera House.

If Walker avoided the controversy of *The Birth of a Nation,* there were still bumps in the road concerning his regard for the theater's black clientele. The segregated balcony, for one, was not a pleasant situation for the blacks. Amid the westerns, comedies, war films, and romances, there were other signs that caste was not as repulsive to Fleet Walker, theater manager, as it had been to M. F. Walker, race theorist. The Opera House stage furthered racial hierarchy, its ads identifying acts as "The Colored Concert Company," or noting that in the Elizabeth Daye Stock Company's great horse-racing play, "a real race horse and colored band used on the stage." A stage presentation of *Uncle Tom's Cabin* appeared in 1916.[47] The greatest indignities, however, continued to accompany the arrival of traveling minstrel shows.

Within two months of one another in 1916 two minstrel shows came to the Opera House. The first, "Mammy's Pickaninny Minstrels," ran a local ad that spelled out the entire program, including the performers' stage names, all degrading stereotypes. A sample: Miss Peach Melba, Mr. Beau Rassick Acid, Miss Ima Cookie, Miss Brown Betty, Miss Etta Pancake, Miss Oleo Margarine, and Miss Honey Drip.[48] The second arrival, "America's Greatest of All Colored Shows," featuring "real colored talent," was even more explicit in tying blacks to their former slave status. It came "direct from the sunny south," and offered "buck and wing dancing" and "plantation scenes." Worst of all, to promote the show, the performing troupe held an afternoon "Koontown parade" in the streets of Cadiz.[49]

If Fleet Walker accommodated these shows either through business necessity or personal callousness, they were reflective of stiffening race relations in the area. Though the Cadiz high school graduated two Negroes in 1916, distance between blacks and whites in the area was pronounced. Interracial social contact was limited to informal mingling in public stores. By 1920 the town had an active Ku Klux Klan chapter that led to at least one local cross burning. Though later the high school, the library, a skating rink, and dances were integrated "to an extent,"[50] much of the tension in Cadiz, as in most places around the country, bubbled below the surface, an endless spring of fear, misinformation, and complicity.

Also roiling below the surface was Fleet Walker's private life. Publicly he was building a reputation among whites as a knowledgeable and respected businessman. The stationery that Walker used heralded the Opera House as having a seating capacity of eight hundred, though a glance at photographs and the building dismiss this figure as inflated self-promotion. In 1915 he had closed a deal with V-L-S-E (the "Big Four" consortium of the film producers Vitagraph, Lubin, Selig, and Essanay) to bring its film-adapted stage spectaculars to the Opera House. Later described as a "weak product" successfully merchandised,[51] V-L-S-E nonetheless had the aura of glamour in Cadiz, and Walker's contract with them hinted at acumen and shrewdness.

But while the Walkers had the look of "solid citizens" with "a lot of gumption" there were details that hinted at the lingering existence of old wounds. While Fleet gave town kids jobs passing out handbills, and sometimes let them into the back seats of the theater for free, he was also known to be moody and could turn irritable if the children made noise in the hallway or accidentally obstructed exiting patrons. As the 1920s approached he also continued to straighten his hair though it had by then thinned to bald patches in the front. Further, Fleet Walker kept occasional company with two white men, attorney Robert Minteer and his friend, O. C. Gray, a University of Michigan graduate; both were tentholders at the annual Chautauqua. Minteer's granddaughter, though a teenager at the time and still lucid about her grandfather, has no recollection of the tall, handsome theater manager. This is not surprising as the friendship involved violating the town's dry codes. Both Walker and Minteer liked to "nip on the bottle," a pastime that would have to be undertaken rather privately.[52]

Within the privacy of the darkened Opera House theater, Fleet Walker was making some other acquaintances, sometimes unknowingly. By 1922 theater exhibitors were using feature films as nearly seventy percent of their attractions,[53] a development that stemmed in part from the rise of film's star system. While once the Opera House had felt graced with visits from travel lecturer Lyman Howe, baseball evangelist Billy Sunday, or the Musical Sullivans, a family that played Swiss bells and xylophones, silent film stars became by 1922 the targets of public demand and devotion and the preferred guests of theatergoers. Their rise had begun as soon as nickelodeons opened and the close-ups of cameras transformed actors into towering figures. After 1915 a cadre of names met with instant recognizability, and all of them paraded across the Opera House screen: Pearl White, Tom Mix, Harold Lloyd, Gloria Swanson; Charlie Chaplin in *The Tramp,* Theda Bara in *The Galley Slave.* Another star sat in the Cadiz theater, enthralled with the likes of Douglas Fairbanks and Mary Pickford. He was not yet a star, of course, because he was still just a teenager. But Clark Gable, of nearby Hopedale, nurtured his aspirations to Hollywood glitter in Fleet Walker's Opera House.[54]

One of the problems that all these stars and their multireel features brought with them was a growing public impatience with time spent waiting for the reels to be changed. When the exotic Poli Negri and a cast of five thousand starred in *Passion,* the Opera House ad promised that the show was on "9 Reels That Seem But 5."[55] Fleet Walker already had an answer to the problem that did not rely on the grand sweep of a film to compress the viewer's sense of time. He invented in the first months of 1920 three improvements for reel loading and changing – a film-end fastener, an entire improved reel, and an alarm for the reel. Previously projectionists either had to wait for a reel to run out or risk setting the film on fire by opening a fireproof door of the film magazine to get a peek. Used in concert, Walker's inventions would help the projectionist alternate two machines efficiently by letting him know exactly when each reel was ending. Walker patented the three inventions in August of that year and, according to the *Cleveland Gazette,* by the following July had negotiated a marketing agreement for them with the Globe Machine and Stamping Company of Cleveland. The paper pronounced the inventions "another substantial victory for the race," and, under a headline that read, "Fleet Walker Scores Big," predicted that the royalties would soon put the former ballplayer on "easy street, financially."[56] It was not to be. Aging and events conspired in the next several years to distance him from the prospect of prosperity.

In 1920 his inventions revealed him as remarkably active for a man in his seventh decade. For ten years he had been outpacing many of the less fortunate among his old acquaintances. When Walker was fifty, Charlie Morton, his former manager with Toledo, had disappeared from Cleveland. When he was found several months later in Chicago, he was suffering from acute dementia and muttering incoherently about Corpus

Christi. Documents in his pockets showed that he had spent time in Texas and Mexico. In the next decade Fleet's family began to yield to time. Simon Merriman died in 1916. Fleet, Weldy, and William helped carry the casket of this brother-in-law who had helped bail Fleet from prison in 1898. Three weeks later, Sarah, Simon's wife and Fleet's sister, passed away. In 1918 brother William died in Wheeling. Finally, on 26 May 1920, Ednah Jane, Fleet's wife of twenty-two years and two weeks, died of chronic nephritis. The illness had been of "long standing and much suffering."[57]

Cadiz took notice of Ednah's death in a lengthy, front-page article. She had been the Grand Matron of the Order of Eastern Star in Ohio and held high positions as well in the Courte of Calanthe and other orders. According to the obituary she had taught school in Canada as well as Kentucky. Personable, intelligent, and efficient, she had, according to the *Democrat-Sentinel,* assisted Fleet as his director and manager. Prof. W. H. Lucas, the husband of a close friend and a leader in the Masonic Lodge, conducted a brief funeral service for Ednah before her remains were taken back to Oberlin for interment. In her decline, the paper stated, "she was lovingly cared for and given every human aid by her devoted husband."[58]

Widowed again, the decline began for Moses Fleetwood Walker. In fifteen years in Cadiz he had overseen a business that went from the occasional circus or band concert to a fifteen minute reel of film to an evening's worth of entertainment in the Opera House that could cost a customer as much as $1.65. A Cadiz newspaper noted in 1922 that it now took four ice cream parlors to cater to the "luxury loving and spending class" of the town.[59] The expenses in accommodating the surging leisure demands swelled also. The cost for ushers, projectionists, advertising, and utilities rose rapidly between 1912 and 1922.[60] Additionally, film rentals from the Cleveland exchange service were now claiming a forty- to fifty-percent share of admission charges.[61] On 1 March 1922, Walker retired, selling the Opera House business to Minteer and Gray.

His announced plans were for several business trips to Dayton, Cleveland, and other cities, followed by at least temporary settlement in Steubenville. The temporary aspect was certainly correct. Less than a month after his retirement, Fleet, accompanied by Weldy, on a return trip from New York City, stopped in Cleveland to consider the leasing of the Temple Theater. When he decided to reenter the theater business, planning a 15 June opening, the *Cleveland Gazette* printed a column trumpeting Walker's theater expertise as well as carrying a large ad that promised "high class motion pictures, road shows, and occasional vaudeville of quality."[62] The *Gazette*'s gushing was predictable. Its editor, the renowned and influential Harry Clay Smith, was an old acquaintance of Fleet's. While still at Oberlin, Ednah had written the lyrics for a song Smith had composed. The editor had hosted both Fleet and Weldy during trips they had made to the city after Ednah's death.[63]

Obviously, Fleet Walker was not ready for retirement. But the Temple Theater, at 2326 East Fifty-fifth Street, ran under Walker's proprietorship for just three months before reverting to prior management.[64] The short-lived venture raises many questions. Why, at age sixty-five, had Walker chosen to start over in Cleveland? Was his desire tied to possible hopes he had for his reel invention? Could there have been greater desires still in him – to invent things, to go to the big city and prove himself? Had he stayed in Cadiz to satisfy Ednah or simply due to inertia? Maybe the constant brushing against screen stars had unconsciously refueled a stalled ambition – or maybe he was going to Cleveland to lose himself.

By this time all of America had stopped "skirmishing with fractional definitions of Negroes." The lessened instances of interracial sex after the turn of the century and the number of blacks marrying among themselves across the complete color spectrum had produced a more homogeneous brown America.[65] In the large city it would be easier for a man of light complexion to find anonymity for his fight with the demons.

If Fleet Walker was looking, on the other hand, for more adventure, it was fortunate that he was no longer enticed by Africa. In 1913 Chief Alfred Charles Sam had begun a scheme that eventually carried sixty poor Oklahoma blacks back to Africa. It also left five hundred behind before collapsing. More recently Marcus Garvey was winning acclaim as the Black Moses, but his lack of business skills was sowing the seeds for forthcoming failure.

Whether he went to Cleveland to nurse ambition or fatigue, Walker clearly found time for reflection. In September 1922 he returned a three-page survey to Oberlin College, which was making a special effort to track down its former students. He listed his occupation as retired. He summed up his Oberlin experience in one underlined word: *excellent.* In the sections given to former occupations and accomplishments, Walker selectively arranged his life. Despite many years with the postal service, he left out his railway clerking altogether, as well as his months as a sewing machine packer. He noted his several inventions in moving pictures, but neglected the registered patent for the guaranteed exploding artillery shell. With what probably combined chronology with an athlete's vanity, he listed first "Professional Base Ball."[66] Still living then at the address of the Temple Theater, Walker was on the same street as and just a trolley hop away from Hooper Field where the Negro National League's Cleveland Browns sometimes played. Had his anger at organized baseball ebbed enough to allow his presence among the spectators there? There is no way to know.

On 11 May 1924 – a Sunday – at 1:25 P.M., Moses Fleetwood Walker passed away. Sick just six hours, he died at his home of lobar pneumonia. Finally, after nearly sixty-seven years, he was free of the question of color. His obituaries bore the marks of his life as he was differently known in his former homes. The *Cleveland Gazette* remembered him as an "oldtime catcher" who was a wonderful batter, runner, and thrower – a "heady" player. Socially he was "affable, genial, intelligent, and deservedly popular."[67] In Cadiz, he was remembered as the motion picture operator, and described by the town's *Cleveland Gazette* correspondent as a "thorough race champion." Steubenville was most aware of his many sides. The *Herald-Star* identified him as one of the best catchers in the nation once, as a player who had fought hotel discrimination, as an ardent advocate in favor of "founding a mighty Black Empire" in Africa, as a U.S. mail employee, as a nickelodeon operator, as a "very interesting man to meet in conversation," and as a prominent colored Mason.[68]

When Fleet Walker died he was once again showing signs of restlessness. He was residing at what was at least his second address in Cleveland – 2284 East Forty-ninth Street – and at least the fourteenth home of his life, an extraordinary number for an era not quite as addicted to mobility as the automobile and airplane would make future decades. When he died there was one final sad truth to add to his story. He was no longer a theater owner, and not a distinguished retired speaker for civil rights as some have proposed. He worked for a man named Percy Owens. Fleet Walker was a clerk in a billiards room.[69]

While two of Fleet's relatives had associations with sport – son George was reported to have once been a boxer and a nephew, William of St. Paul, Minnesota (probably the son of either Cadwallader or William), was a noted bicycle rider – the other Walkers seemed more seduced by the lure of gaming and drinking. Weldy Wilberforce Walker lived with his nephew Thomas at the Union Hotel until he died in 1937, of influenza. In the years of Prohibition he had become a bootlegger.[70] Thomas, Fleet's son, and proprietor of the Union Hotel and its billiards parlor, was known as a generous and kind man. But in addition to having oil interests, he also became a bookmaker, though he left the field after failing to pay off on a numbers game.[71] When he died the hotel inventory revealed that the business had been more involved with the exchange of money than with the comfort of lodgers. It included just five single beds and five springs, but three adding machines and two cash registers.[72] When Thomas died in 1939 following complications in a goiter operation, an investigation revealed that though he had once been wealthy, he was now deeply in debt. His wife, Jeannette, was forced to move to Lima, Ohio, and live off the charity of a distant relative.[73]

Upon Fleet's passing, Weldy, Thomas, and a white friend, Mr. McLister, went to Cleveland and brought his body back to Steubenville to be buried next to his first wife, Arabella. The funeral service was held at Thomas's home at 321 South Third Street.[74] Cleodolinda Walker Mills, his daughter then living in Pasadena, California, son George, and sister Sarah were reported as survivors in obituaries, but there was no mention that they had attended the services. If not, it would have been just one more oddity in a lifetime of paradox.

At birth, there was the mystery of the possible twin, and, of course, the unknown provenance of the bloodlines. At Oberlin College he had proved himself an anomaly, a scholar who angled for a career among professional athletes. As a baseball player whose survival depended in part on invisibility, he played the most prominent of all positions with flair. As a gun carrier, knife wielder, and mail robber he was a shocking blot on the nearly spotless record of the mulatto elite (a study done in 1932 on 2,537 mulattos born after 1860 found that only *one* was ever known to have been arrested – Walker had quadrupled that on his own). As a black separatist he was a man who could not abide white society's shunning of merit but could never bring himself to actually separate from white society. As a theater operator he had conspired with an industry that promoted the idea of black inferiority. As a man of society he was a convivial conversationalist held hostage by a violent temper, and as a father he produced offspring whose ambitions regrettably settled far beneath his own. Perhaps his own father would have said that the son never fulfilled the powerful promise of the name. Finally, in death, he was buried in an elaborate, beautiful casket, but left no will. This Wednesday's child had figuratively taken a turn with every day of the week and exhausted them all.

. . . .

... then the days of weeping and

mourning for Moses were ended.

Deuteronomy 34.8

EPILOGUE

Except for its suddenness, Moses Fleetwood Walker's death lacked the cinematic flair that his extraordinary life seemed to demand. My yearning as a biographer and romantic had spawned imaginings in which Fleet died running toward some unknown destination, overtaxing a heart that was falling apart after decades of failed dreams and hopelessness. But most humans eventually yield to the formlessness of reality, become incapable of a fitting and final drama of their own making. In Fleet Walker's case, the living have always been willing to keep constructing it for him. Arthur Ashe, another black "first" who died nearly seventy years later (also of pneumonia as the immediate cause) knew Walker's story and included him in his three-volume history of the black athlete. Jackie Robinson knew of Walker. Many baseball fans know him only as a trivia answer.

Bits and pieces of his life are still around, though you have to look closely for them. Baseball's Hall of Fame, in Cooperstown, New York, includes a small tribute to Walker in an exhibit that honors the blacks excluded from competing with whites during the years of the color barrier. *Our Home Colony* is among the listed holdings of the rare manuscript division of the Library of Congress, though it has been missing from inventory for over a decade. The best path for those who wish to partake in the ongoing discovery of irony and myth in Fleet Walker's story winds through many places that he tried to – and probably desperately needed to – call home. It begins where he ended.

Steubenville, Ohio, in the late twentieth century has the look of a fading industrial town that is trying valiantly to survive in a culture whose symbols of adaptation are fast-food chains. Unemployment there is high, and over the last twenty years a number of buildings have been torn down in favor of empty spaces. Still, drive into town from the west and you will pass the Taco Bell, the Pizza Hut, and the Bob Evans restaurant – evidence of survival. It would be a mistake to assume that Steubenville's determination to keep up implies the lack of a historical consciousness. Its stately mansions further downtown and its elegant courthouse with the memorial to native Edwin Stanton, Abraham Lincoln's Secretary of War, hint that this is not a place with an uninteresting past. It is just that the demands of living amid the transition from hardscrabble industry to a service economy have peopled the area with many for whom the exigencies of life are the uncertainties of labor and the powerful high-school football team. Many of its residents, echoing Moses Fleetwood Walker, think that life would be a simpler proposition if the races could somehow live separately. There is, understandably then, no Fleet Walker Street in Steubenville. There is, however, a Sunset Boulevard – a salute to Hollywood's Dean Martin, another Steubenville native – and near its intersection with Hollywood Boulevard, a visitor can find Fleet Walker. Rubbing elbows once more with the improbable duo of celebrity and invisibility, he lies buried there in Union Cemetery.

In the early 1980s a visitor needed a map and a willing caretaker to find lot V in section P where the unmarked graves of Fleet, Weldy, Arabella, Fleet's son, Thomas, and his infant grandson, Thomas Jr. are located. Stepping gingerly around the gravesite in this strikingly lovely cemetery is the most unsettling of the turns encountered along Walker's historical path. What is Walker doing in this place opened to accommodate Civil War dead? Why unmarked graves? A modest but dignified headstone would have cost only about $75 in 1924. The lid of his casket alone cost nearly that much. The casket proper went for an extravagant $525. Because Fleet Walker left no will it is plausible that his son Thomas, who helped Weldy to bury Fleet, paid for the casket. Or maybe the unmarked grave was a way to seek final quietude, to admit that more ambitious schemes had brought no solace. Perhaps Fleet's final irony was to fulfill the white perception of mulattos as "invisible" people – to leave behind not a trace. If so, it did not work. In 1990 Oberlin College's John Heisman Club inducted Fleet Walker into their Hall of Fame and placed a stone on his grave. It is hard to know how Walker would have liked it. The headstone identifies him as the nation's first black major leaguer, reducing a vivid life to achievement born partly of accident and partly of the caste system he so adamantly fought. The back identifies the Heisman Club as the stone's donor. The ceremony that accompanied its placement led to a search for Walker's successors. Right there in Steubenville, the hunt turned up Dennis Palmer, Jr., the grandson of Sarah Merriman, one of Fleet's sisters. He attended the ceremony along with his sister, Sarah Palmer Freeman.

Leave Union Cemetery and drive downtown. Dr. Moses W. Walker's address at 313 South Street is a vacant lot, though across the street, Grant Junior High School, built in 1868 as the colored school, still stands. The Union Hotel at 107 Market Street, near the courthouse, is gone and replaced. Closer to the Ohio River and the spot where runaway slaves stepped onto free soil, there is an alley still identified as Lake Erie Avenue. It now connects nothing to nothing. There is, however, taking shape on a huge vacant lot there, a reconstructed version of Fort Steuben, a compound that is part of the modern era's attempt to tap into tourism and roots through the clever arrangement of concrete and factory-milled, rough-hewn wood into pseudoplaces. Though the Walker brothers proposed to lead their African emigration from an address on Lake Erie Avenue, there will probably be little interest in recreating a Liberian colonization office on the site. Disharmony lacks tourist appeal.

Backtracking next to Cleveland it seems more possible that Walker was, by the end of his years, trying to find home not in a locale but in a state of mind. Or maybe he had given up on a home in search of something else. The big city and the willful abandonment of responsibility have combined to shroud more than one broken heart in anonymity. It is less easy here than in Steubenville to sort the urban decay from what was once urban renaissance. There is little of either to admire on East Fifty-fifth Street. Hooper Field, site of Negro baseball, is no longer a relic in fact or memory – just gone like it was never there. Not surprisingly, 2326 East Fifty-fifth, Fleet's address in 1922 and the site of the Temple Theater when he returned his Oberlin College questionnaire, now houses one two-story sliver of a sprawling brick project that contains some of Cleveland's poorer residents. Strangely enough, despite greater impersonality it is in Cleveland that one senses the connection between Fleet Walker's life and modern America. Large cities have so little quaintness and are naturally given to so much pretense to progress that events that just missed touching his life, when thought about here, seem to be but a short reach from our own: Malcolm X's birth in 1925; the conviction of Marcus Garvey in the month of Fleet's death for – of all things – mail fraud; Rube Foster and his entrepreneurial Negro major league; the suntan as status symbol for whites; one of Clark Gable's first film appearances in *The Merry Widow;* the preoccupation with firsts.

In Cadiz, Ohio, the connection becomes palpable. There are several people one can talk to here who actually knew Fleet and Ednah Walker. In the early 1980s, their opera house became, in another coincidence, a sporting goods store. But even now, as a carved up office and apartment space, it is recognizable as a former opera house. Though the telltale Gothic arches of the original windows are walled in, the color difference between old brick and new still traces their former splendor. Unlike many small towns that have redesigned downtown storefronts in willful efforts to create a charming past they never had, Cadiz has simply let time have its due. The town doggedly maintains, however, its pursuit of dignity, refusing to budge on its century-old ban on alcohol. Still, if you stood in the street between the Harrison County Courthouse and Walker's opera house and threw a boomerang, it would hit a half-dozen illegal speakeasies during its trip home. Cadiz seems contented and, even as a county seat, far removed from the grit of Steubenville or the bustle of Cleveland. It is easy, nonetheless, to imagine the considerable importance it had seventy years ago and Fleet Walker's contribution to the town's modern life.

Of all Fleet Walker's former homes, Oberlin, just an hour's drive southwest from Cleveland, knows him best. The Moses Fleetwood Walker file in the archives at Oberlin College has grown noticeably thicker in the past decade, filled as the result of the work and inquiries of baseball researchers who have written nearly twenty articles on Walker. The archivists are all quite familiar with his story. The Oberlin athletic department also knows Walker. In 1913 the college failed to select him to its All-Time Baseball Team, but in 1990 the John Heisman Club put him in the school's athletic Hall of Fame. As with many small colleges which once jousted briefly with the giants, Oberlin's athletic prowess faded in the twentieth century to a status more reflective of its noted academic and social reputations. In the early 1970s, however, Oberlin briefly grabbed the attention of the sports world when it hired radical Jack Scott to revamp the athletic department. His vision included nonauthoritarian coaches (one of whom was Tommie Smith, a participant in the famed black power salute on a 1968 Olympic victory platform), self-reliant athletes, and joy of movement. The attempt to reify the vision did not last long. The effort was so repulsive to the nation's athletic establishment that Ohio State's legendary football coach, Woody Hayes, included the school in one of his legendary tirades. Calling Scott a "pipsqueak," Hayes said, "I'd like to get that goddamn Oberlin on our schedule! We'd show them what *de*-humanization is all about." In many ways, Oberlin College continues to fight dehumanization, though, sadly, in the 1990s it struggles like the rest of society to stay ahead. Many of its black students reside in a segregated African heritage dormitory.

This continuing miasma of de facto race separation and the scholarly insistence upon separate American experiences according to race continue to create for the biographer the delicate task of sifting meaning through the sieve of color. What sent Fleet Walker to jail – character or color? What lifted the bottle to his lips? Some of these things we can only know intuitively; all answers are unwelcome. It is small wonder that most Walker researchers have taken up Alex Haley's charge to "find the good and praise it." This is understandable to a degree. But the good, as Haley knew, shines brightest when placed next to the bad, or, as Maxim Gorky put it in *Childhood:* "our life is amazing not only for the vigorous scum of bestiality with which it is overgrown, but also for the bright and wholesome creative forces gleaming beneath."

A little of Fleet Walker's creative gleaming was left behind in all the places he called home. While it is too painful to look at the corner of Orange and Monroe in Syracuse, the Justin cannons on the shore of Oneida Lake are reminders of his mechanical ingenuity. It is easy to see moviehouses in Newark and old ball fields in Toledo and be reminded of his ambition, ability, and affability. The same is true of Gallipolis and Ann Arbor and New Castle and Waterbury – all offer fleeting wisps of Walker's universal search for fulfillment. But the truest sense of Moses Fleetwood Walker comes from his first home.

In Mount Pleasant, Ohio, things still seem closest to what they must have been like in 1857. The large Quaker meeting hall, built in 1814, stands well maintained, a historical landmark that still casts a shadow down the hill and over the spot where Moses W. Walker's house stood, where Cadwallader was raised, and Fleet and Lizzie Walker were born. Mount Pleasant speaks of a time before the nation became obsessed with recordkeeping, a time when people, like Cadwallader and Lizzie, were still allowed to slip away leaving barely a smudge across the public record. But the public record is not the only means for stretching the threads of a person's life across time.

In the sheltered environs of rural eastern Ohio, the fame and celebrity that attach to being a landmark baseball player pale next to the more important and intimate matters of family trees and bloodlines. Knowledge and suspicions of these intimacies still circulate among the people, unwritten links between each other, the larger world, and the past. Not surprisingly, the guarded and disputatious lore on Moses Fleetwood Walker, seventy years after his death, whispers that he once fathered a son by a white mistress who lived in West Virginia. Raised as a white, the son went on to become a member of the West Virginia legislature. The roll of legislators does not produce any confirming names, and the threads that run back toward the possibility are so thin as to be invisible. Indeed much of Fleet Walker's life bears the same inclination toward invisibility. He has never been an easy man to know. Past writings about him have gotten so much of the simple wrong – including his mother's name, his wife's name, his daughter's name, his birth date, his occupations, and even his own name – that it is little wonder that deeper matters of the soul have yielded the same numbing platitudes and sometimes just silence.

It is appropriate, then, that in the hidden hills of Mount Pleasant, a place where reality takes precedence over carefully constructed public image and possibilities become inextricable from plausibilities and improbabilities, that Fleet Walker seems most vivid. Here the Walker family is united. Drive out of town, round a bend or two, and they all disappear, family and village, nothing left but the mind's picture and an eerie sense of time travel that recedes with the miles and the reappearance of the interstate highway. It is in the mind's perceptions rather than in the restored and sometimes recreated artifacts of the past that Moses Fleetwood Walker finally attains the status he deserves as an immeasurable and imperishable human presence.

APPENDIX 1

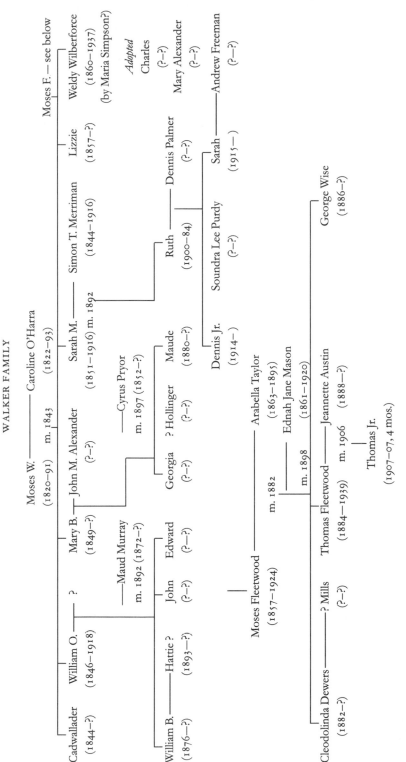

WALKER FAMILY

EJane Mason

APPENDIX 2

· · · · · · · · · · · · ·

Moses Fleetwood Walker's Professional Baseball Statistics

Year	Club	League	Games	Runs	Hits	Batting Ave.	Slugging Pct.	Position	Errors	Fielding Pct.
1883	Toledo	Northwestern League	60	45	59	.251	.353	catcher	78	.783
1884	Toledo	American Association	42	23	40	.263	.316	catcher	37	.887
1885	Cleveland	Western	18	11	19	.279	.441	catcher	na	na
	Waterbury	Eastern	10	5	6	.154	.154	catcher	4	.960
	Waterbury	Southern New England	na	na	na	na	na	catcher, outfield	na	na
1886	Waterbury	Eastern	47	23	37	.218	na	catcher, outfield, first base	37	.895
1887	Newark	International League	69	44	67	.264	.315	catcher	31	.945
1888	Syracuse	International Association	77	38	48	.170	na	catcher	45	.919
1889	Syracuse	International	50	29	37	.216	.234	catcher	29	.865

Courtesy Jerry Malloy.

NOTES

INTRODUCTION

1. Greil Marcus, *Mystery Train: Images of America in Rock and Roll Music* (New York: E. P. Dutton, 1975), 146–47.

2. Gerald Early, "Their Malcolm, My Problem," *Harper's Magazine* 285 (Dec. 1992): 72.

1. EARLY MOSAIC

1. *Oberlin Review* 8 (23 Oct. 1880): 33; Harry D. Sheldon to C. W. Savage, 19 Dec. 1934, Moses Fleetwood Walker file, Oberlin College Archives.

2. Marriage records of Jefferson County OH, 5: 231.

3. Entry for Moses Walker, Warren Township, Jefferson County, OH, Seventh Census of the United States, 1850, records of the Bureau of the Census, record group 29, National Archives, Washington DC, 200; entry for Moses Walker, Steubenville, Jefferson County, OH, Eighth Census of the United States, 1860, 236.

4. James L. Burke and Donald E. Bensch, *Mount Pleasant and the Early Quakers of Ohio* (Columbus: Ohio Historical Society, 1975), 17.

5. Charles L. Blockson, *The Underground Railroad* (New York: Prentice Hall, 1987), 206.

6. Wilbur Henry Siebert, *The Mysteries of Ohio's Underground Railroads* (Columbus OH: Long's College Book Co., 1951), 300.

7. Burke and Bensch, *Mount Pleasant,* 30–32.

8. Siebert, *Mysteries,* 4.

9. "Pioneer Days," *Steubenville Herald,* n.d., from the files of the Historical Society of Mt. Pleasant OH.

10. Joseph B. Doyle, *Twentieth Century History of Steubenville and Jefferson County, Ohio* (Chicago: Richmond-Arnold, 1910), 489.

11. *Encyclopedia of American Quaker Genealogy,* vol. 41 (Ohio), ed. William W. Hinshaw (Baltimore: Genealogical, 1973).

12. Entry for Moses Walker, Steubenville, Jefferson County OH, Ninth Census of the United States, 1870, 6; entry for Mary B. Pryor, family 128, Enumeration District 129, Youngstown, Mahoning County OH, Thirteenth Census of the United States, 1910.

13. Entry for Moses Walker, Canonsburg, Washington County PA, Fifth Census of the United States, 1830, 237; entry for Moses Walker, North Station, Washington County PA, Sixth Census of the United States, 1840, 52; entry for Moses Walker, Brunswick County VA, Sixth Census of the United States, 1840, 337; entry for Moses Walker, Enumeration District 110, Steubenville, Jefferson County OH, Tenth Census of the United States, 1880, 32.

14. Entry for Thomas F. Walker, Enumeration District 217, Steubenville, Jefferson County OH, Fourteenth Census of the United States, 1920, 1; certificate of death for Welday W. Walker, 27 Nov. 1937, Ohio Department of Health, Division of Vital Statistics, file no. 69927, Jefferson County; certificate of death for Moses Fleetwood Walker, 11 May 1924, file no. 27001, Jefferson County.

15. Entry for Moses Walker, Tenth Census of the United States, 1880.

16. An unidentified newspaper article, ca. 1944, in a personal scrapbook of a Cadiz OH resident, cited Ralph E. LinWeber's *Toledo Baseball Guide of the Mud Hens: Directory of History Records Indicating Sixty Years of the Toledo Baseball Club, 1883–1943* (Rossford OH, 1944), and LinWeber himself as sources for a brief but inaccurate description of Fleet Walker's life.

17. G. Jahoda, "A Note on Ashanti Names and Their Relationship to Personality," *British Journal of Psychology* 45 (1954): 193, cited by Mechal Sobel, *The World They Made Together: Black and White Values in Eighteenth Century Virginia* (Princeton NJ: Princeton Univ. P, 1987), 154.

18. Sharon M. Hymer, "What's In a Name?" *Dynamic Psychotherapy* 3 (fall-winter 1985): 186–97.

19. Eugene Genovese, *Roll, Jordan, Roll: The World the Slaves Made* (New York: Vintage Books, 1974), 252–54.

20. *Two Hundred Years of U.S. Census Taking: Population and Housing Questions, 1790–1990* (U.S. Dept. of Commerce, Bureau of the Census, 1990), 26.

21. *Louisville Courier-Journal*, 22 Aug. 1881; "Pioneer Days," *Steubenville Herald*, n.d., from the files of the Historical Society of Mt. Pleasant OH.

22. John G. Mencke, *Mulattoes and Race Mixture: American Attitudes and Images, 1865–1918* (Ann Arbor: UMI Research Press, n.d.), ix.

23. Ibid., 57.

24. Carl Vogt, *Lectures on Man* (1864), 183–92, cited by Stephen Jay Gould, *The Mismeasure of Man* (New York: W.W. Norton, 1981), 103.

25. Horace Bushnell, *Christian Nurture* (1860), cited by George M. Fredrickson, *The Black Image in the White Mind: The Debate on Afro-American Character and Destiny, 1817–1914* (New York: Harper and Row, 1971), 155–56.

26. Gould, *Mismeasure*, 35.

27. David Gerber, *Black Ohio and the Color Line, 1860–1915* (Urbana: Univ. of Illinois P, 1976), 249.

28. Fredrickson, *Black Image*, 78.

29. Ibid., 185.

30. Mencke, *Mulattoes*, 54–55; Joel Williamson, *New People: Miscegenation and Mulattoes in the United States* (New York: Free Press, 1980), 92.

31. Mencke, *Mulattoes,* 6; Barbara Jeanne Fields, "Slavery, Race and Ideology in the United States of America," *New Left Review* 181 (May/June 1990): 103–6.

32. Genovese, *Roll,* 458.

33. Fredrickson, *Black Image,* 89, 188.

34. Mencke, *Mulattoes,* 38; Williamson, *New People,* 94–95.

35. Richard Harrison Shryock, *Medical Licensing in America, 1650–1965* (Baltimore: Johns Hopkins Univ. P, 1967), 32–33; William G. Rothstein, *American Physicians in the Nineteenth Century: From Sects to Science* (Baltimore: Johns Hopkins Univ. P, 1972), 75–76.

36. Entry for Moses Walker, Eighth Census of the United States, 1860.

37. Gerber, *Black Ohio,* 63, 56.

38. D. T. McConnell, *Steubenville: Past, Present and Future* (Cleveland: Reifsnider and Kemp, 1872), 18; Doyle, 395; *Cleveland Gazette,* 7 May 1910, 1.

39. *Chicago Inter Ocean,* cited by the *Terre Haute Express,* 24 July 1890, 2.

40. Entry for Moses Walker, Ninth Census of the United States, 1870. This census entry is the only one to record the inability of Caroline Walker to read or write.

41. William E. Bigglestone, *Oberlin: From War to Jubilee, 1866–1883* (Oberlin OH: Grady, 1983), 57; *Oberlin Weekly News,* 27 July 1876, 25 Jan. 1877, 29 Mar. 1878.

42. Entry for Moses Walker, Ninth Census of the United States, 1870.

43. *Oberlin Weekly News,* 4 Jan. 1878, 24 May 1877.

44. Frederick Davis Shults, "The History and Philosophy of Athletics for Men at Oberlin College" (Ph.D. diss., Indiana Univ., 1967), 17–27.

45. *Catalogue of the Officers and Students of Oberlin College, For the Year 1879–80* (Oberlin OH: Mattison's Steam Printing House, 1879), 56–61.

46. Ibid., 45.

47. Ibid., 44–48; Moses Fleetwood Walker transcript, records of the Office of the Registrar, Oberlin College Archives, book 12, 266.

48. *Steubenville Herald,* 22 Oct. 1869, 3, cited in Timothy Michael Matheney, "Heading for Home: Moses Fleetwood Walker's Encounter with Racism in America" (bachelor's thesis, Princeton Univ., 1989), 11.

49. *Oberlin Weekly News,* 28 June 1877.

50. Shults, 28.

51. J. J. Shipherd, *Circular: Oberlin Collegiate Institute,* 8 Mar. 1834, cited by Shults, 31.

52. W. C. Cochran, "Historical Sketches of Athletics at Oberlin College," *Oberlin Alumni Magazine* 10 (Feb. 1914), 130–31, cited by Shults, 64.

53. Shults, 41.

54. *Oberlin Review* 8 (23 Oct. 1880), 31.

55. Harlan F. Burket, "Biographical Notes of My Mother and Father," Harlan F. Burket Papers, MSS 641, box 1, notebook 1, Ohio Historical Society Archives, Columbus OH.

56. Ibid.; Burket, "My College Life at Oberlin," MSS 641, notebook 2, Burket Papers.

57. Burket, "Biographical Notes," "My College Life." An apocryphal parallel

story of the twentieth century has the legendary Negro League pitcher Satchel Paige instructing a skeptic to stand behind a tree while Paige hits him with his "optical illusion."

58. Burket, "My College Life."

59. "Catalogue and Records of Colored Students, 1834–1972," vol. 1, Oberlin College Archives.

60. Burket, "My College Life."

61. Henry Churchill King, "The Primacy of the Person in College Education," 1903 inaugural address, Oberlin College, cited by Shults, 162–63.

62. James B. Angell to James Harris Fairchild, 7 Mar. 1882, Fairchild Papers, box 5, Oberlin Archives.

63. A. T. Packard, Ann Arbor, Mich., to Fairchild, 17 Mar. 1882, Fairchild Papers, box 5.

64. Fairchild, *Moral Science,* 281, cited by Shults, 159.

65. Entries for Moses Walker, Eighth Census of the United States, 1860; Ninth Census of the United States, 1870.

2. INTO THE FIRE

1. *Oberlin Review* 8 (25 June 1881), 239.

2. Bigglestone, "Oberlin College and the Negro Student, 1865–1940," *Journal of Negro History* 56 (July 1971): 200–1; Willard B. Gatewood, *Aristocrats of Color: The Black Elite, 1880–1920* (Bloomington: Indiana Univ. P, 1990), 251.

3. C. Vann Woodward, *The Strange Career of Jim Crow,* 3d rev. ed. (New York: Oxford Univ. P, 1974), 16–35.

4. *Louisville Courier-Journal,* 22 Aug. 1881.

5. *University of Michigan Chronicle* 12 (30 June 1881), 267; 13 (4 Mar. 1882), 150.

6. *Oberlin Review* 9 (22 Apr. 1882).

7. *Michigan Chronicle* 13 (27 May 1882), 226; 13 (10 Sept. 1882), 253.

8. John Behee, *Hail to the Victors* (Ann Arbor: Ulrich's, 1974), 41–43; statistics sheet compiled by Karl Wingler, ca. 1960, in the Moses Fleetwood Walker file, National Baseball Hall of Fame and Museum, Cooperstown NY. Wingler lists just five games, but the *Michigan Chronicle* of 10 Sept. 1882 recorded six Michigan victories, two against each of its league opponents: Racine, Madison, and Northwestern.

9. Certificate of marriage, Michigan Department of Health, record no. 1398, in Moses Fleetwood Walker file, Oberlin College Archives; *Steubenville Daily Herald,* 12 June 1895, 8.

10. Burket, MSS 641, box 2, folder 6, Burket Papers.

11. *New Castle Daily City News,* 15 July 1882, 1; 26 July 1882, 4.

12. Harry D. Sheldon to C. W. Savage, 19 Dec. 1934, Moses Fleetwood Walker file, Oberlin College Archives.

13. Burket, "My College Life."

14. *Pittsburg Leader,* cited in *New Castle Daily City News,* 19 Sept. 1882, 1.

15. *New Castle Daily City News,* 28 Mar. 1882, 4.

16. *New Castle Daily City News,* 4 Aug. 1882, 4.

17. *New Castle Daily City News,* 28 Aug. 1882, 4; 29 Aug. 1882, 3.

18. *New Castle Daily City News,* 9 Sept. 1882, 3; 15 Sept. 1882, 4.

19. Harvey Green, *Fit for America: Health, Fitness, Sport and American Society* (New York: Pantheon, 1986), 7–8, 316–17.

20. *Steubenville Herald-Star,* 19 Sept. 1898; *Michigan Chronicle* 14 (9 June 1883), 263.

21. Samuel L. Clemens, *Mark Twain's Speeches* (New York: Harper, 1923), 145.

22. *Columbus Ohio State Journal,* 23 Apr. 1883, 4.

23. Mencke, *Mulattoes,* 39.

24. Williamson, *New People,* 96.

25. Burket, MSS 641, box 2, folder 6, Burket Papers.

26. *Sporting Life,* 23 July 1884, 7.

27. *Toledo Blade,* 8 May 1883, 3; 23 May 1883, 3; Burket, MSS 641, box 1, 2.

28. *Oberlin News-Tribune,* 28 Dec. 1945.

29. William A. Brewer, "Barehanded Catcher," *Negro Digest* (Oct. 1951), 86.

30. *Toledo Blade,* 4 Sept. 1883, 3.

31. David Q. Voigt, *American Baseball: From Gentleman's Sport to the Commissioner System,* vol. 1 (Norman: Univ. of Oklahoma P, 1966), 175, 177.

32. *Sporting Life,* 22 July 1883, 7, cited by Larry Bowman, "Moses Fleetwood Walker: The First Black Major League Baseball Player," *Baseball History: The Annual of Original Baseball Research,* ed. Peter Levine (Westport CT: Meckler Books, 1989), 65.

33. *Cleveland Gazette,* 9 Aug. 1884, 4.

34. *Sporting Life,* 22 July 1883, 7.

35. *Toledo Blade,* 27 Apr. 1883, 3; 17 July 1883, 3.

36. *Toledo Blade,* 30 Apr. 1883, 3; 21 June 1883, 3; 19 Sept. 1883, 3.

37. *Columbus Ohio State Journal,* 23 Apr. 1883, 4.

38. *Cleveland Gazette,* 22 Sept. 1883, 4; 13 Oct. 1883, 2; 27 Oct. 1883, 1; 8 Dec. 1883, 3; *Oberlin News-Tribune,* 28 Dec. 1945.

39. *Toledo Blade,* 11 Aug. 1883.

40. Ibid.

41. *Sporting Life,* 15 July 1883, 7.

42. *Sporting Life,* 15 Oct. 1883, 6.

43. Voigt, *American Baseball,* 127–28.

44. *Toledo Blade,* 15 Apr. 1884, 3.

45. *Louisville Commercial,* 27 Apr. 1884, 1; 30 Apr. 1884, 2; 1 May 1884, 4.

46. *Louisville Commercial,* 2 May 1884, 2.

47. *St. Louis Globe-Democrat,* 2 May 1884, 8; 22 May 1884, 8; *Baltimore Sun,* 5 June 1884, 4.

48. *Sporting Life,* 24 Sept. 1884, 3.

49. John A. Brown to C. H. Morton, 11 Apr. 1884, Walker file, Oberlin College Archives.

50. Lonnie Wheeler, "Hounded Out of Baseball," *Ohio* 16 (May 1993), 26.

51. *Toledo Blade,* 22 May 1884, 3; 23 May 1884, 3, cited by Matheney, "Heading for Home," 44.

52. *New York Age,* 11 Jan. 1919, cited by Ocania Chalk, *Pioneers of Black Sport* (New York: Dodd, Mead, 1975), 8.

53. *Cleveland Gazette,* 19 July 1884, 1.

54. Fredrickson, *Black Image* 95–96.

55. *Sporting Life,* 9 Apr. 1884, 4.

56. Bill James, *The Baseball Book, 1990* (New York: Villard Books, 1990), 247–52.

57. "The Future of the Negro," *North American Review* (July 1884): 83–84, cited by Fredrickson, 228–29.

58. *New York Times,* 12 May 1884, 1.

59. *Sporting Life,* 1 Oct. 1884, 2.

60. *Sporting Life,* 23 July 1884, 7; 6 Aug. 1884, 7; 1 Oct. 1884, 5.

61. *Cleveland Gazette,* 13 Dec. 1884, 2; 31 Jan. 1885, 2.

62. *Cleveland Gazette,* 4 Oct. 1884, 3.

63. *Steubenville Daily Herald,* 21 Oct. 1884, 1.

64. *Cleveland Gazette,* 24 Jan. 1885, 1.

65. *Steubenville Daily Herald,* 25 Oct. 1884, 3.

66. *Cleveland Gazette,* 24 Jan. 1885, 1; 31 Jan. 1885, 1.

67. *Cleveland Gazette,* 31 Jan. 1885, 1.

68. *Cleveland Gazette,* 10 Jan. 1885, 1.

69. *Sporting Life,* 4 June 1884, 6.

70. *Toledo Blade,* 16 July 1884, 3; 17 July 1884, 3; 24 Sept. 1884, 3, cited by Matheney, 40.

3 . WITHOUT A WORLD TO CONQUER

1. *Toronto Daily Mail,* 14 May 1888, 2.

2. *Toronto Daily Mail,* 24 May 1888, 2; *Toronto Globe,* 24 May 1888, 3; *Sporting Life,* 6 June 1888, 9; *Toronto Daily Mail,* 26 May 1888, 4.

3. *Cleveland Plain Dealer,* 8 Apr. 1885, 4; 22 Apr. 1885, 2.

4. *Memphis Daily Appeal,* 15 Apr. 1885, 1; *Atlanta Journal,* 14 Apr. 1885, 1.

5. *Sporting Life,* 8 Apr. 1885, 3; 15 Apr. 1885, 5.

6. *Sporting Life,* 29 Apr. 1885, 7; *Cleveland Plain Dealer,* 21 Apr. 1885, 3.

7. *Cleveland Plain Dealer,* 1 May 1885, 8; *Sporting Life,* 8 Apr. 1885, 3; 15 Apr. 1885, 3.

8. *Sporting Life,* 6 May 1885, 7; 13 May 1885, 7; 27 May 1885, 7; Steven Riess, *Touching Base: Professional Baseball and American Culture in the Progressive Era* (Westport CT, Greenwood, 1980), 124.

9. *Sporting Life,* 1 July 1885, 7, cited by Matheney, "Heading For Home," 56.

10. *Waterbury Daily Republican,* 5 Aug. 1885; 29 Sept. 1885.

11. *Cleveland Gazette,* April 1886, cited by Chalk, *Pioneers,* 14–15; *Cleveland Gazette,* 14 Mar. 1885, 1; *Cleveland Gazette,* 5 Dec. 1885, cited by Chalk, 14.

12. Jerry Malloy, "Moses Fleetwood Walker," in *Nineteenth Century Stars,* ed.

Robert L. Tiemann and Mark Rucker (Manhattan, KS: Society for American Baseball Research, 1989), 131.

13. Peterson, *Only the Ball*, 34–39; *Cleveland Gazette*, 5 Mar. 1887, 1.

14. *The Sporting News*, 18 June 1887, 4.

15. *Cleveland Gazette*, 13 Feb. 1892, 1.

16. *Newark Daily Journal*, 24 Mar. 1887.

17. *Newark Daily Journal*, 29 July 1887.

18. *Sporting Life*, cited by Malloy, "Out at Home," in *The Armchair Book of Baseball II*, ed. John Thorn (New York: Chas. Scribner's Sons, 1987), 267.

19. *Newark Daily Journal*, cited by Malloy, "Out at Home," 267.

20. *Newark Daily Journal*, 5 Apr. 1887; Malloy, 267, 272–73.

21. *Newark Daily Journal*, 8 Apr. 1887; 14 Apr. 1887.

22. *Newark Daily Journal*, 14 Apr. 1887; 3 Sept. 1887.

23. *Newark Daily Advertiser*, 26 Apr. 1887, 1.

24. *The Sporting News*, 18 June 1887, 4.

25. Cited by Malloy, "Out At Home," 273.

26. *Newark Evening News*, 15 July 1887, 3.

27. Peterson, *Only the Ball*, 29.

28. Matheney, "Heading for Home," 61; *Newark Daily Journal*, 8 Apr. 1887; Malloy, "Out at Home," 272.

29. *Cleveland Gazette*, 17 May 1924, 2.

30. *Newark Daily Journal*, 16 July 1887.

31. *Sporting Life*, 20 July 1887, 1.

32. See Barry Kessler and David Zang, *The Play Life of a City: Baltimore's Recreation and Parks, 1900–1955* (Baltimore: Baltimore City Life Museums, 1989), 31–41.

33. *Newark Daily Journal*, 7 July 1887.

34. *Terre Haute Express*, 1 July 1890, 1.

35. *Cleveland Gazette*, 12 Apr. 1884, 2.

36. *Newark Daily Journal*, 26 May 1887.

37. *Toronto World*, cited in *Newark Daily Journal*, 18 June 1887; *Newark Daily Journal*, 2 July 1887.

38. *Newark Daily Journal*, 26 Nov. 1887, 3.

39. *Newark Daily Journal*, 8 Aug. 1887; 25 Nov. 1887; *Sporting Life*, 18 Jan. 1888.

40. *Sporting Life*, 24 Aug. 1887; *Newark Daily Journal*, 9 Sept. 1887.

41. *The Sporting News*, 10 Dec. 1887, 4.

42. *Newark Daily Journal*, 29 Nov. 1887.

43. Malloy, "Out At Home," 274.

44. Ibid., 275–76.

45. Ibid., 278.

46. *Toronto Daily Mail*, 17 May 1888, 2.

47. *New York Age*, 13 Oct. 1888, cited by Matheney, "Heading for Home," 69.

48. *Syracuse Courier*, 9 July 1888, 8.

49. Matheney, "Heading for Home," 67–68; Malloy, "Out At Home," 276, 283.

50. *Toronto Daily Mail,* 24 May 1888, 2; *Sporting Life,* 30 July 1884, 7; *Newark Daily Journal,* 5 Sept. 1887.

51. *Sporting Life,* 3 Oct. 1888, 1.

52. *Sporting Life,* 2 Jan. 1889, 2.

53. *Sporting Life,* 6 Feb. 1889, 1.

54. John R. Husman, "Major League Baseball First For Toledo," *Metropolitan* (July–Aug. 1988), 56–57.

55. *Cleveland Gazette,* 7 Sept. 1889, 1.

56. Malloy, "Out At Home," 284.

57. Ibid., 269.

58. *Sporting Life,* 1887, cited by Malloy, "Out At Home," 271.

59. *Terre Haute Express,* 3 Aug. 1890; 4 Aug. 1890; 29 July 1890.

60. *Sporting Life,* 14 Mar. 1888, 5.

4 . SUNLIGHT TO DARKNESS

1. *Columbus Ohio State Journal,* 23 Apr. 1883, 4.

2. *Syracuse Courier,* 10 Apr. 1891, 4.

3. Ibid.

4. *New York Times,* 27 May 1890; 28 May 1890.

5. Letters Patent no. 458,026, United States Patent Office, Crystal City VA; *Syracuse Courier,* 1 Apr. 1891, 5.

6. *Steubenville Daily Herald,* 1 Oct. 1891.

7. *Cleveland Gazette,* 17 Oct. 1891, 1.

8. *Cleveland Gazette,* 28 Nov. 1903, 1.

9. Gatewood, *Aristocrats of Color,* 9–10, 23, 182, 208.

10. Ibid., 173.

11. *Cleveland Gazette,* 30 Jan. 1909, 1.

12. Mencke, *Mulattoes,* 61.

13. Gatewood, *Aristocrats of Color,* 17.

14. *Cleveland Gazette,* 18 Apr. 1891, 1.

15. *Syracuse Courier,* 10 Apr. 1891, 4.

16. *Syracuse Courier,* 11 Apr. 1891, 5.

17. Ibid.

18. *Syracuse Daily Journal,* 13 Apr. 1891.

19. *Syracuse Courier,* 13 Apr. 1891, 5.

20. *Syracuse Daily Journal,* 9 May 1891, 4.

21. *Syracuse Courier,* 2 June 1891, 5.

22. Entry for Addison Lewis, vol. 85, Enumeration District 83, Jefferson County OH, Twelfth Census of the United States, 1900, records of the Bureau of the Census, record group 29, National Archives, Washington DC, 14; entry for Harrison L. Hoyt, vol. 15, E.D. 2, Onandaga County NY, Twelfth Census of the United States, 1900, 3.

23. *Cleveland Gazette,* 18 Apr. 1891, 1.

24. *Syracuse Daily Journal,* 9 May 1891.

25. *Syracuse Courier,* 2 June 1891, 5; *Syracuse Daily Journal,* 2 June 1891, 2.

26. *Syracuse Daily Journal,* 4 June 1891, 2; *Syracuse Courier,* 4 June 1891, 4.

27. *Syracuse Courier,* 3 June 1891, 4; *Syracuse Daily Journal,* 3 June 1891, 2.

28. *Syracuse Courier,* 4 June 1891, 4; *Syracuse Daily Journal,* 3 June 1891, 2.

29. *Syracuse Daily Journal,* 4 June 1891.

30. Ibid.

31. Seymour Sacks with Robert Sacks, *The Syracuse Black Community* (Syracuse: Syracuse University's Maxwell School of Citizenship and Public Affairs, 1987), 10, 35.

32. *Cleveland Gazette,* 13 June 1891, 2.

33. *Cleveland Gazette,* 23 May 1891, 1.

34. Marriage records of Jefferson County OH, vol. 8, 422; "Pioneer Days."

35. *Steubenville City Directory* (Akron: Burch Directory Co., 1892–93).

36. *Steubenville Daily Herald,* 19 June 1891.

37. *Steubenville City Directory* (1892–93); *Steubenville Daily Herald,* 6 July 1916; marriage records of Jefferson County OH, vol. 12, 458.

38. *Cleveland Gazette,* 17 Mar. 1894, 2; 27 July 1895, 1.

39. *Deaths Recorded in Jefferson County, 1888–1898,* (2-258-301).

40. Ibid. (2-288-97).

41. 1894 Oberlin College questionnaire, student file of Ednah Jane Mason, Oberlin College Archives; necrology for the year 1919–20 from Moses Fleetwood Walker file, Oberlin College Archives; *Cadiz Democrat Sentinel,* 3 June 1920, 1; entry for Pat Mason, reel 1235, Lorain County OH, Ninth Census of the United States, 1870, records of the Bureau of the Census, record group 29, National Archives, Washington DC, 19; entry for Pat Mason, vol. 40, E.D. 180, Tenth Census of the United States, 1880; interview with Marcella Ballard, Cadiz OH, Sept. 1992; telephone interview with James Johnson, Cadiz OH, 20 Jan. 1993.

42. A. R. Holmes and A. P. Owens to W. J. Vickery, Cincinnati, 20 Sept. 1898, record group 28, records of the Post Office, Case Files of Investigations, Nov. 1877–Dec. 1903, entry 231, *U.S. v. Moses F. Walker,* National Archives, Washington DC.

43. Ibid.

44. *Steubenville Herald-Star,* 22 Sept. 1898, 5.

45. *Steubenville Weekly Gazette,* 23 Sept. 1898.

46. Record group 21, record of the District Court of the United States, Southern District, Eastern Division (Columbus), criminal case no. 275, *U.S. v. Moses F. Walker,* National Archives, Great Lakes Region, Chicago.

47. *Steubenville Weekly Gazette,* 7 Oct. 1898; 28 Oct. 1898.

48. *Steubenville Weekly Gazette,* 23 Sept. 1898; record group 21, case no. 275, *U.S. v. M. F. Walker.*

49. Entry for David Darrah, vol. 11, E.D. 17, Belmont County, Ohio, Twelfth Census of the United States, 1900, records of the Bureau of the Census, record group 29, National Archives, Washington DC, 3; entry for Robert Love, vol. 85, E.D. 77, Jefferson County OH, Twelfth Census of the United States, 1900, 13.

50. *Steubenville Weekly Gazette,* 16 Dec. 1898.

51. Verdict, Final Commitment, *U.S. v. Moses F. Walker,* record group 21, National Archives, Great Lakes Region, Chicago.

52. *Steubenville Herald-Star,* 14 Dec. 1898, 4.

53. Record group 204, record of pardon cases, volume S, Department of Justice, National Archives, Washington DC, 85.

54. Record group 28, case files of investigations, entry 231, *U.S. v. Moses F. Walker,* National Archives, Washington DC.

55. *Journal of the American Medical Association* 20 (7 Jan. 1893): 1–2; Mencke, *Mulattoes,* 59.

56. *Ohio State Journal,* 13 Dec. 1898; 14 Dec. 1898.

57. Entry for Wilbur E. King, vol. 63, E.D. 81, Franklin County OH, Thirteenth Census of the United States, 1910, records of the Bureau of Census, record group 29, National Archives, Washington DC.

58. Mencke, *Mulattoes,* 144; Williamson, *New People,* 100–3.

59. *Reach's Official Base Ball Guide* (Philadelphia, 1896), 139.

60. Steve A. Martin, "The Passing of Anson," *Sporting Life,* 26 Feb. 1898, 9.

5. CHAMADE

1. *Cleveland Gazette,* 30 Oct. 1897; Ocania Chalk, *Pioneers of Black Sport* (New York: Dodd, Mead, 1975), 13; Gerber *Black Ohio,* 358–59.

2. *Cleveland Gazette,* 29 Aug. 1891, 1.

3. Adrian C. Anson, *A Ball Player's Career* (Chicago: Era, 1900), 148–50.

4. *The Sporting News,* 1 Apr. 1899.

5. Mencke, *Mulattoes,* 49, 84–105.

6. Ibid.

7. Entry for Fleet Walker, dwelling no. 443, Steubenville, Jefferson County OH, Eleventh Census of the United States, 1900, records of the Bureau of the Census, record group 29, National Archives, Washington DC.

8. See for example the *Indianapolis Freeman,* 21 Nov. 1903; the *Richmond Planet,* 3 Oct. 1897; *Colored American Magazine,* 12 Mar. 1898; the *Cleveland Gazette,* 8 Apr. 1905.

9. *New York Times,* 19 June 1905, 12.

10. *Colored American Magazine,* 12 Mar. 1898.

11. File no. 2237 of the Office of the Assistant Attorney General for the Post Office Department, 1905, record group 28, records of the Post Office, National Archives, Washington DC; file no. 2254, Attorney General of the Post Office, 1906, record group 28.

12. Ad for M. B. Berger and Co., *Colored American Magazine* 15 (Feb. 1909), 186.

13. *Cleveland Gazette,* 8 Apr. 1905.

14. Wilson J. Moses, *The Golden Age of Black Nationalism, 1850–1925* (Hamden CT: Archon Books, 1978), 11.

15. See Phillips Verner Bradford and Harvey Blume, *Ota Benga: The Pygmy in the Zoo* (New York: St. Martin's, 1992).

16. W. E. B. Du Bois, *The Conservation of Races* (Washington DC, 1897), 16–17.

17. *Steubenville City Directory* (Akron: Burch Directory Co., 1895–96, 1899–1900, 1902–3, 1904–5, 1906).

18. Ibid., 1902–3; Weldy Walker, reply to Oberlin College General Catalogue of Former Students, 15 July 1908; and Moses F. Walker's reply to Oberlin inquiry of former students, Sept. 1922, both in the Moses Fleetwood Walker file, Oberlin College Archives.

19. "Pioneer Days."

20. Edwin S. Redkey, *Black Exodus: Black Nationalist and Back-to-Africa Movements, 1890–1910* (New Haven: Yale University Press, 1969), 16.

21. M. F. Walker, *Our Home Colony: A Treatise on the Past, Present, and Future of the Negro Race in America* (Steubenville OH: Herald, 1908), 31.

22. Miles Mark Fisher, "Deep River," *Negro Slave Songs in the United States* (New York: Citadel Press, 1969), repr. in *Black Brotherhood: Afro-Americans and Africa,* ed. Okon Edet Uya (Lexington MA: D. C. Heath, 1971), 12.

23. Ibid., pref.

24. Redkey, *Black Exodus,* 18.

25. P. J. Staudenraus, *The African Colonization Movement, 1816–1865* (New York: Columbia Univ. P, 1961), 246.

26. *Cleveland Gazette,* 18 July 1891, 1.

27. *Apropos of Africa: Sentiments of Negro American Leaders on Africa from the 1800s to the 1950s,* ed. Adelaide Cromwell Hill and Martin Kilson (London: Frank Cass, 1969), 4.

28. Staudenraus, *African Colonization,* 244.

29. *Apropos,* 163.

30. Alexander Crummell, "The Relations and Duties of Free Colored Men in America to Africa" (1 Sept. 1860), in *Black Brotherhood,* 65.

31. *Apropos,* 73–77.

32. August Meier, *Negro Thought in America, 1880–1915* (Ann Arbor: University of Michigan Press, 1964), 63, 66.

33. Bishop H. M. Turner, 12th letter, Monrovia, Liberia, 5 Dec. 1891, in *Apropos,* 238.

34. E. D. Cope, "The Return of the Negroes to Africa," *Open Court* 4 (12 June 1890): 2331.

35. Redkey, *Black Exodus,* 280–81.

36. Weldy Walker questionnaire, Moses Fleetwood Walker file, Oberlin College Archives.

37. Unidentified newspaper clipping, 2 Mar. 1992, from files of Harrison County Historical Society, Cadiz OH; *Cleveland Gazette,* 11 Aug. 1908, 1; *Steubenville Herald-Star,* 9 Sept. 1908.

38. Walker, *Our Home Colony,* 4.

39. Ibid., 46.

40. Ibid., 6.

41. Ibid., 7.

42. Ibid., 31.

43. Ibid., 39.

44. Ibid., 21.

45. Ibid., 20.

46. Ibid., 34.

47. Ibid., 18–19.

48. Ibid., 7–8.

49. Ibid., 26.

50. Ibid., 28.

51. Ibid., 6–7, 31–32.

52. Williamson, *New People,* 116–17.

53. Walker, *Our Home Colony,* 27.

54. Ibid., 36.

55. Ibid., 43.

56. Fredrickson, *Black Image,* 294.

57. Walker, *Our Home Colony,* 7, 43.

58. Ibid., 28, 44.

59. Ibid., 28, 43.

60. Ibid., 44–45.

61. Ibid., 46.

62. Ibid., 44.

63. Gatewood, *Aristocrats of Color,* 170.

64. Walker, *Our Home Colony,* 27–28.

65. Ibid., 44.

66. Ibid., 27.

67. Ibid., 29.

68. Ibid., 25.

69. Ibid., 22.

70. Ibid., 21.

71. Ibid., 41.

72. Ibid., 10, 39.

73. Ibid., 39.

74. Record group 59, records of the Department of State, Index to Passport Applications, 1906–23, box no. 94, National Archives, Suitland MD.

75. Walker, *Our Home Colony,* 35.

6. END CREDITS

1. *Steubenville City Directory* (1899–1900, 1902–3, 1904–5, 1906).

2. *Steubenville City Directory* (1904–5, 1906, 1908, 1909, 1911, 1913, 1915–16, 1918, 1921, 1924, 1926, 1928, 1931–32, 1933–34, 1936–37); entry for Cyrus M. Pryor, E.D. 129, Youngstown, Mahoning County OH, Twelfth Census of the United States, 1910, records of the Bureau of the Census, record group 29, National Archives, Washington DC, 128.

3. *Cleveland Gazette,* 8 Mar. 1902, 1; 29 Mar. 1902, 2; 12 Apr. 1902, 2; 21 June 1902, 2.

4. Richard Koszarski, *An Evening's Entertainment: The Age of the Silent Feature Picture, 1915–1928,* vol. 3 of *History of the American Cinema,* ed. Charles Harpole, 3 vols. (New York: Charles Scribner's Sons, 1990), 201.

5. Charles Musser, *The Emergence of Cinema: The American Screen to 1907,* vol. 1 of *History of the American Cinema,* 15.

6. Ibid., 39–82.

7. Ibid., 109.

8. Ibid., 9.

9. Ibid., 393–417.

10. Ibid., 428.

11. Cadiz newspaper clippings from a theater file at the Harrison County Historical Society, Cadiz OH, 4 Oct. 1906; 11 Oct. 1906; 26 Sept. 1907; 3 Oct. 1907; 22 Apr. 1909; 27 May 1909; 3 Feb. 1910; 11 Apr. 1912; 21 Nov. 1912.

12. Ibid., 10 Dec. 1908.

13. Musser, *Emergence,* 430–33; Eileen Bowser, *The Transformation of Cinema, 1907–1915,* vol. 2 of *History of the American Cinema,* 8–11.

14. Lin Weber, *Toledo Baseball Guide,* 20.

15. Bowser, *Transformation,* 38–40.

16. Ibid., 2.

17. *Cadiz Sentinel,* 6 May 1915, 2.

18. Ibid., 14 July 1904, 2.

19. Ibid., 13 Oct. 1910.

20. Ibid., 27 Jan. 1910, 2.

21. Doyle, *Twentieth Century History of Steubenville,* 274.

22. Interview with Ballard, Oct. 1992.

23. Ibid.

24. Musser, *Emergence,* 292, 380.

25. Interview with Ballard; interview with Johnson.

26. Ibid.

27. *Cleveland Gazette,* 2 Apr. 1910, 1.

28. *Cleveland Gazette,* 1 Feb. 1902, 2; 25 Dec. 1909, 1.

29. *Cadiz Republican,* 8 July 1909, 2; *Cadiz Sentinel,* 8 July 1909.

30. *Cleveland Gazette,* 23 Apr. 1910, 2.

31. Musser, *Emergence,* 193.

32. Record group 9, mayoral papers, J. Barry Mahool, S.14, no. 398, Baltimore City Archives.

33. Randy Roberts, *Papa Jack: Jack Johnson and the Era of White Hopes* (New York: The Free Press, 1983), 112.

34. *Cadiz Republican,* 7 July 1910, 3.

35. *Cadiz Republican,* 19 Dec. 1910.

36. Bowser, *Transformation,* 10.

37. Ibid., 21.

38. Newspaper clippings, theater file, Harrison County Historical Society, 15 Aug. 1912; 19 Sept. 1912; 21 Nov. 1912.

39. Ibid., 4 Sept. 1913; 11 Sept. 1913.

40. Bowser, *Transformation,* 19.

41. Newspaper clippings, Harrison County Historical Society, 19 Sept. 1912; 20 Feb. 1913.

42. Ibid., 2 Mar. 1922.

43. Musser, *Emergence,* 15.

44. Thomas R. Cripps, "The Reaction of the Negro to 'Birth of a Nation,'" *The Historian* 25 (May 1963): 344–59.

45. Ibid.

46. Interview with Johnson; interview with Esther Clark, Sept. 1992, Bowerston OH.

47. *Cadiz Democrat-Sentinel,* 18 Mar. 1915; 4 Nov. 1915, 2; 23 Mar. 1916.

48. Ibid., 7 Sept. 1916.

49. Ibid., 9 Nov. 1916, 3.

50. Interview with Ballard.

51. *Cadiz Democrat-Sentinel,* 4 Nov. 1915; Bowser, *Transformation,* 74.

52. Interviews with Ballard, Johnson, Esther Clark; telephone interview with Ruth Minteer. The observation on "nipping on the bottle" was made under request for anonymity.

53. Koszarski, *An Evening's Entertainment,* 9.

54. Clark Gable to Harry McConnell, 6 May 1948, from the collections of the Harrison County Historical Society, Cadiz, Ohio.

55. *Cadiz Republican,* 12 Jan. 1922, 4.

56. Letters patent, nos. 1,328,408; 1,348,609; and 1,345,813; 20 Jan. 1920, United States Patent Office, Crystal City VA; *Cleveland Gazette,* 2 July 1921.

57. *New York Times,* 17 Mar. 1909, 5; *Chicago Tribune,* 17 Mar. 1909, 8; *Steubenville Daily Herald,* 6 July 1916; 27 July 1916; 28 Sept. 1918; *Cadiz Democrat-Sentinel,* 3 June 1920, 1.

58. *Cadiz Democrat-Sentinel,* 3 June 1920, 1.

59. *Cadiz Republican,* 26 Jan. 1922, 2.

60. Koszarski, *An Evening's Entertainment,* 14.

61. Interview with Clark.

62. *Cleveland Gazette,* 10 June 1922.

63. Ibid., 26 July 1884; 2 July 1921, 3; 1 Apr. 1922.

64. Ibid., 16 Sept. 1922.

65. Williamson, *New People,* 127.

66. Moses F. Walker file, Oberlin College Archives.

67. *Cleveland Gazette,* 17 May 1924, 2.

68. Ibid., 17 May 1924, *Steubenville Herald-Star,* 13 May 1924, 3.

69. *Cleveland City Directory* (The Cleveland Directory Co., 1924), 2736, 2090.

70. Interview with Johnson.

71. Telephone interview with Dennis Palmer Jr., Oct. 1992.

72. Jefferson County, Ohio Administrative Docket, vol. 14, 317.

73. Ibid.

74. *Steubenville Daily Gazette,* 14 May 1924, 5.

BIBLIOGRAPHICAL ESSAY

Capturing Fleet Walker's many sides and interests required looking at sources diverse in both nature and topic. My reconstruction of his family and personal life leaned on several sources. Personal interviews with Walker's grandnephew and three people who actually knew him in Cadiz, Ohio, yielded descriptions of his appearance, temperament, and to a lesser extent his habits of thought and behavior. The official records – census, marriage, birth, death, probate – were useful for information on relationships, race, occupations, estate, literacy, and family roots. The records of the post office, State Department, Department of Justice, and the patent office were crucial in confirming his inventiveness, for which he took credit, and his criminal problems, on which he was understandably mute.

After Walker enrolled at Oberlin College his life became more public. The Oberlin College Archives is a rich mine for Walker material including: college newspapers and alumni publications, catalogs, baseball scorebooks, photographs, grade transcripts, letters, returned surveys, necrologies, directories, and, of course, Walker's *Our Home Colony*. Additionally, the archivists have done a fine job of collecting the secondary material that researchers have contributed. The Moses F. Walker file has become a fascinating read in itself.

Also very useful for understanding Walker's Oberlin experience was William E. Bigglestone's *Oberlin: From War to Jubilee, 1866–1883* (Oberlin 1983), Frederick D. Shults's doctoral dissertation, *The History and Philosophy of Athletics for Men at Oberlin College* (1967), and former Walker teammate Harlan Burket's remarkably detailed diaries at the Ohio State Historical Society, in Columbus.

Other institutions that have accumulated helpful files on Walker are the Harrison County Historical Society, in Cadiz, Ohio, and the Jefferson County Historical Society in Steubenville. Also in Steubenville, the Schiappa Library maintains easily accessible directories from a hundred years ago, microfilm of the Steubenville papers, and old histories of Jefferson County.

Of the more than thirty newspapers consulted, the *Cleveland Gazette* stands out as a guide to what many of the black elite were thinking and doing across a long stretch of years. The *Gazette* also made frequent mention of the Walker family in small items that revealed some of their social and business activities, travels, and whereabouts over the course of more than three decades.

Walker's baseball days are the most heavily documented aspect of his life,   149 though not always the most interesting. Daily newspapers were the best sources of his performance, though regrettably there were few black newspapers to take note of his major league season in Toledo. In particular, the *Toledo Blade,* the *Newark Daily Journal,* the *Syracuse Courier,* and, of course, *Sporting Life* and *The Sporting News* were more extensive in their coverages than most others. While on baseball I should mention that the provenance for this biography and a great many other studies involving black baseball are found in Robert Peterson's outstanding *Only the Ball Was White* (Englewood Cliffs NJ 1970). Two other books gave me important and well-written looks at a black athlete under duress: Randy Roberts's *Papa Jack: Jack Johnson and the Era of White Hopes* (New York 1983), and Jules Tygiel's *Baseball's Great Experiment: Jackie Robinson and His Legacy* (New York 1983).

While my file of secondary articles on Walker is bulging, most accounts are brief, one-sided rehashes on the theme of "black man made bitter by his baseball experience." A small bunch of writings resist this obvious simplification. The best of them are Jerry Malloy's "Out At Home," found in the John Thorn-edited anthology, *The Armchair Book of Baseball II* (New York 1987); Timothy Michael Matheney's undergraduate thesis for Princeton University, "Heading for Home: Moses Fleetwood Walker's Encounter With Racism in America" (1989); and Donald Lankiewicz's "Fleet Walker in the Twilight Zone," from *Queen City Heritage* (summer 1992).

Trying to avoid the limited perspective inherent in "first-black" studies, I was greatly informed and enriched in the complexities of color, class, and the idea of race by a number of good works. Of greatest impact was the recent and highly controversial work of Barbara Jeanne Fields, "Slavery, Race and Ideology in the United States of America," which appeared in the May/June 1990 issue of the *New Left Review.* While its assertions are uncomfortable, they are also intelligent and undeniably worthy of deep consideration. On the issue of slavery and its impact, there are, of course, many fine books. I found Eugene Genovese's *Roll, Jordan, Roll: The World the Slaves Made* (New York 1974) the most useful still. John G. Mencke's *Mulattoes and Race Mixture: American Attitudes and Images, 1865–1918* (Ann Arbor, n.d.), Joel Williamson's *New People: Miscegenation and Mulattoes in the United States* (New York 1980), and George M. Fredrickson's *The Black Image in the White Mind: The Debate on Afro-American Character and Destiny, 1817–1914* (New York 1971) provided my framework for the issue of race mixing and the difficulties that mulattos faced. All three volumes were outstanding. Stephen Jay Gould's acclaimed *The Mismeasure of Man* (New York 1981) provided a vital record of the graphic and visible affronts of "scientific" racism. David A. Gerber's *Black Ohio and the Color Line, 1860–1915* (Urbana IL 1976) was a good source of detail for Ohio situations, and C. Vann Woodward's *The Strange Career of Jim Crow* (New York 1980) remains unmatched in relating the shifts in attitudes in Americans after Emancipation and Reconstruction.

Willard B. Gatewood's *Aristocrats of Color: The Black Elite, 1880–1920* (Bloomington IN 1990) and August Meier's *Negro Thought in America, 1880–1915* (Ann Arbor 1964) are good accounts of the thoughts, motives, and actions of the influential black leaders – business, political, religious, and social – between 1880 and 1920, important here because Walker had one foot in their world at most times.

He also had one foot outside their world, pointed toward Africa. Six books were particularly valuable in exploring the topics of black nationalism and the possibilities of an African return: a compilation of primary documents edited by Adelaide Cromwell Hill and Martin Kilson and titled, *Apropos of Africa: Sentiments of Negro American Leaders on Africa from the 1800s to the 1950s* (London 1969); William E. Bittle and Gilbert Geis's *The Longest Way Home: Chief Alfred C. Sam's Back-to-Africa Movement* (Detroit 1964); *Black Brotherhood: Afro-Americans and Africa*, edited by Okon Edet Uya (Lexington MA 1971); Edwin S. Redkey's *Black Exodus: Black Nationalist and Back-to-Africa Movements, 1890–1910* (New Haven CT 1969); P. J. Staudenraus's *The African Colonization Movement, 1816–1865* (New York 1961); and Wilson J. Moses's *The Golden Age of Black Nationalism, 1850–1925* (Hamden CT 1978).

Finally, in assessing Walker's final career as a theater operator, I could not have gone far without Scribner's outstanding series, History of the American Cinema, which is constituted by these three chronologically arranged volumes: Charles Musser, *The Emergence of Cinema: The American Screen to 1907* (New York 1990); Eileen Bowser, *The Transformation of Cinema, 1907–1915* (New York 1990); and Richard Koszarski, *An Evening's Entertainment: The Age of the Silent Feature Picture, 1915–1928* (New York 1990).

INDEX

drinking, 47, 60, 79, 113; as editor of *The Equator*, 95–96; embezzlement charge, 82–86; and finances, 37, 52, 58, 59–60, 61, 85–86; and fraternal societies, 81, 115; in Gallipolis OH, 100; interest in law, 26, 32, 50–51; in major leagues, 39–47; marriages, 29, 82; motion picture technology, invention of, 110, 121, 123; with Newark club, 53–56; with New Castle PA club, 29–32; at Oberlin College, 1–2, 16–26, 123; physical appearance, 8, 34, 64, 76, 78, 92–93; as postal employee, 45, 67–68, 81, 82–86, 88; physical demands on and injuries, 36–37, 44–45, 49, 58; racial ideology, 33, 62–63; racial incidents while playing baseball, 27–29, 38–39, 41–44, 54, 61; salary as professional baseball player, 37, 52, 59–60; significance of name, 6–8; in Steubenville OH, 14–15, 45–46, 81, 95–96, 107; status as mulatto, 2, 8, 28, 34–35, 53, 76, 79, 87, 92, 115; and Sunday baseball issue, 50–51; with Syracuse tars, 48–49, 58–61; Syracuse stabbing: 66, 71, 72–80; after Syracuse, 67; as theater owner and entrepreneur, 51–52, 60, 95–96, 109–23; with Toledo club, 35–45, 47; treatment by press, 28–29, 37–38, 41–42, 45, 49, 51, 54, 58; and University of

Michigan, 22–23, 29, 32, 51; with Waterbury CT club, 51–52

Walker, Moses W. (father): background, 5, 6, 8; birth, 2; death, 81; involvement with issues of race, 6, 14, 16; marriage, 3; occupations and status, 3, 14, 15–16

Walker, Sarah M. Merriman (sister), 3, 81, 122, 125, 128

Walker, Thomas Fleetwood (son), 6, 35, 37, 87, 95, 107–8, 124, 125, 127

Walker, Thomas Jr. (grandson), 127

Walker, Weldy Wilberforce (brother), 105, 123, 125; activism, 45–46, 62–63, 90, 96–97, 100; background, 5–6, 8, 15; death, 124, 127; as collegian, 22, 24, 32; in professional baseball, 31, 45, 52; in Steubenville, 45–46, 81, 95, 107–8, 122

Walker, William (nephew), 124

Walker, William O. (brother), 3, 6, 15, 46, 81, 95, 122

Ward, John Montgomery, 55, 63

Washington, Booker T., 95, 96, 105

Welch, Curt, 43

Weld, Theodore, 8

Welday, Alexander, 8

White, Sol, 55

White Sewing Machine Company baseball club, 27–28

Wilberforce, William, 8

Wilson, Woodrow, 118

World's Fair, St. Louis (1904), 94, 96

Wright, Charles, 74